# ENGLAND'S EASTENDERS

# ENGLAND'S EASTENDERS

## FROM BOBBY MOORE TO DAVID BECKHAM

**RICHARD LEWIS**

MAINSTREAM
PUBLISHING
EDINBURGH AND LONDON

First published in Great Britain in 2002 by
MAINSTREAM PUBLISHING COMPANY (EDINBURGH) LTD
7 Albany Street
Edinburgh EH1 3UG

ISBN 1 84018 499 X

A catalogue record for this book is available from the British Library

Typeset in Caslon and Meta Book

Printed in Great Britain by
Creative Print and Design Wales

To Hayley, Rachel and Samuel for bringing
the sunshine into my life . . . and to the
memory of Nana Sadie

# Acknowledgements

There are so many people I must thank for sparing the time to see me or speak to me on the telephone in my pursuit of writing *England's Eastenders*.

None more so than my good friend and colleague Duncan Mackay, the athletics correspondent of *The Guardian* and *Observer* newspapers, for actually clicking my brain into gear with the idea that I should put together this story of my experiences of football in the east end into book form.

The people I have written about in the book I cannot thank enough for allowing me into their thoughts and reminiscing on some of their great days when they were in pursuit of achieving a football dream, or talking about the people who are part of the story.

Of those not mentioned in the book, I must thank the following: Leon Angel, Steve Bacon, David Barber, Nick Bitel, David Bloomfield, Ian Chadband, Nigel Clarke, Ian Cole, Bryn Cooper, John Cross, Tony Banks, David Barber, Jeff Farmer, Paul Johnson, Anthony Kane, Maxine Leckerman, Steve McKenlay, Kevin Moseley, Paul Newman, Vikkie Orvice, Matt Porter, Ian Rathbone, Jack Steggles, Michelle Wassell, Janice Whitlock, Neil Wilson, John Wragg, and friends and colleagues at the *Guardian–Gazette* and *Ilford Recorder* newspapers.

Thank you to my parents for allowing me back into my old room to work in the quiet of a temporary office, to Mum for reading every word and suddenly becoming a football fan – and to Dad for allowing Mum to read every word while you had to cook for a week.

And to my wife Stacey for making the spelling corrections that were needed!

Thank you,

Richard

# Contents

# Foreword

FOOTBALL IN THE EAST END OF LONDON IS VERY DEAR TO ME, not so much because of the position I now hold at Leyton Orient but because of my memories of the area. In 1959 I saw my first match, standing on the terraces at Orient's Brisbane Road ground when they played Scottish side Falkirk in a friendly game. It was a draw and immediately I decided to model myself on the Orient striker Tommy Johnston. From that day on, he was my hero and in the next match I played, there I was, bustling like him, more robust than ever.

I lived in Debden in Essex and Orient was on the London Underground's central line if I wanted to go to watch a football game. I used to attend games on my own and my mum and dad did not mind because Orient always had this reputation of being a safe, friendly, warm club, right up until the present day. I make sure of that.

But it is amazing the mix of people who come to watch football and the fact that it is a game where the class divide can become irrelevant among the true fans.

My greatest story from my time watching football in east London came at Orient when I was standing on the terraces next to an ordinary guy who was wearing a cloth cap. We started chatting and he asked me what I was doing that evening. I told him I was going to the cinema to see *Antony and Cleopatra*, one of the first true classic films to come out of Hollywood. He said I should stay to see the credits at the end, and to look out for the name of the costume designer, because it was his daughter, Edith Head.

I looked at him like he was mad: a guy standing on the terraces at

Orient had connections in Hollywood!

When the film was over, I waited for the credits and there was the name, Edith Head; she progressed to become the main costume designer for the whole of Hollywood, working on such epics as *The Ten Commandments* and *Ben Hur*, yet her dad lived in a terraced house in Leyton and went to watch Orient. That's football and the east end for you.

While I transferred my allegiance to Tottenham Hotspur in time for their Double-winning season of 1960–61, I still went to Orient. But I will never forget one time at Spurs when, before the game, all the youngsters ran onto the pitch to get the players' autographs. As I was heading towards Dave Mackay, by mistake he kicked the ball straight at me and sent me flying backwards. Now Dave was such a hard player and he came up to me and asked me if I was OK. I said: 'Yes, I am fine, Mr Mackay, and can I have your autograph?' He replied: 'No, now go away!'

Thirty-odd years later I was at a football dinner. Dave was there, and I went up to him, told him the story and said: 'May I have your autograph now, please?'

I used to play on Hackney Marshes – who didn't from around our way? The amount of players who have progressed from this part of the world into professional football is amazing, but areas can do that to people: there was a drive and aspiration established after the end of the Second World War – it was upwards from then on.

When Orient came to me asking for my involvement and knowing my past, I went back there with trepidation. But once I walked in, saw the directors' box and looked over to the terraces where I used to stand, the memories came flooding back. That was in 1996 and my first game as chairman was fantastic. My daughter was in the directors' box with me and she said: 'This is great, Dad, it is like having your own Subbuteo team.'

I told her I might be a hero today but it will not always be like that. But the important thing is to ensure we have great fun, because that is the way football is supposed to be.

I spend much of my time abroad but I work my diary around the home games and attempt to get to as many of the away matches as I possibly can. But I am a great believer in developing the young, local talent. Lower-division clubs are an essential part of communities and perhaps the government should think more about putting extra into teams in each area: every MP has a local team.

We have a first-team squad of 22, of which 11 or so are local lads we have brought through the system. So, the east end is still producing players, and you never know, we might have some true stars of the future.

*Barry Hearn,*
*sports entrepreneur and*
*chairman of Leyton Orient*
*Football Club, 2002*

## 1. Full of Eastern Promise

WE FIRST MET ON A SUNNY SATURDAY AFTERNOON. IT WAS NOT so much a blind date as an unexpected liaison; perhaps a dangerous one. Twenty-five years on, we are still together. There have been good times and bad times, more bad than good, but you see it through; you do not give up just because of what happens on one day. We have been through a cavalcade of emotions. I have done most of the shouting and sometimes I have got a response. Not always. Most times they have not listened, just got on with doing it their way – not always the best way.

My dad is to blame. He introduced us, though he did not know too much about it. One of those things: a spare Saturday afternoon, a bit of matchmaking.

In fact, he did not even see the romance blossom. He fell asleep and by the time he woke up, I knew it was love.

Well, not so much love, more deep affection. You know the type. You would love to leave but all the time you would be thinking about them, wondering what they were doing, how they were getting on, would they be missing you? In fact it is easier to stay. Less guilt.

I remember the date clearly. Saturday, 17 September 1977.

Here I am, sitting in row A, seat 22, B block and there they are. Well, there they are in my memory because this is a Tuesday afternoon now. By the kind generosity of a few people, I have been allowed in to reminisce back to an age of innocence when I had no intention of committing myself for life, before discovering I had already done so.

I have not been to this spot for 20 years, but the passage of time is a good friend and I can recall the moment that kick-started it all.

A good ball to the edge of the box, a poor defensive clearance and a volley from the full-back, a rip-snorter of a shot from 25 yards that flew through the air with the power, pace and direction of an Exocet missile. The ball rocketed into the top corner and from then on, I knew I did not want to watch my football anywhere else but here in the east end of London.

Row A, seat 22, B block. That is where it happened. Dad missed most of it because he was not a football fan: he had taken me to shut me up and he was so bored, he was close to snoring.

In 25 years, not much has changed at Brisbane Road.

I did not know it at the time but Saturday, 17 September was the start of a wonderful journey. So where better a place to begin than here at Leyton Orient Football Club, my dear companion, for a quarter of a century and the inspiration that has led me to take you on this tour around the east end of London, a part of the capital of England that has developed a production line of footballing superstars that, arguably, cannot be matched, whichever corner of the world you care to mention.

Beaches in Brazil, grasslands in Germany, sunshine of Spain: go on, have a go. Not one stretch of any country can lay claim to have produced such a constant succession of footballers as this one, players that have not just allowed the world to stand up and take notice but have changed the way the beautiful game is perceived.

Aptly, the story starts in the year and month I was born: July 1966. It is World Cup time in England and the legend of Bobby Moore is being carved into our nation's history.

Moore was England's greatest captain, perhaps its greatest player, an ambassadorial figure for the game. He reached heights that no England player has experienced again, lifting the World Cup after victory against West Germany in the final at Wembley, and then returning home to his modest semi-detached house in a road in Ilford in Essex on the outskirts of the east London border, five streets away from where I was welcomed into the world.

I made sure I told Bobby where I lived the first time I met him in

August 1980, when he arrived to present the prizes at his soccer school, where I had been seconded to prevent another seven days of summer holiday monotony. He shook my hand and stood chatting for a moment, congratulating me on my efforts (three goals in a week and one stupendous save) and then, as we waited to get the bus home, he drove out, waved, stopped and apologised for not being able to give me a lift because he had another appointment. They say everyone who was ever in his company has a story about Bobby Moore, and this one was mine.

Fast-forward six years to my first day as sports editor of a newspaper in north-east London. It was 1986, and I was hardly in my seat when the telephone rang. It was a representative from the Trustee Savings Bank (TSB) asking me if I would like to spend the forthcoming weekend in Manchester as a guest at the final of a competition called the Bobby Charlton Soccer Skills developed from his soccer school. TSB were the sponsors, and they were inviting a selection of local reporters to accompany the boys from their areas who had reached the final.

Wow. What a way to start in a new position. Of course I would go. Oh, and by the way, what was the boy's name from my area? I asked.

There was a long pause on the line as the TSB man went down his list, and I could hear him rustling through the pages, checking the anonymous name of the local youngster I would be travelling to Manchester with.

'He's from Chingford,' said the man. 'His name is David Beckham.'

Fifteen minutes of fame, eh? I can safely say that I was the first journalist ever to write the two most famous words in world football today. The following Monday, after we had returned from Manchester, I was typing out 'David Beckham' in much the same way as his name now finds itself in print: in glowing lights. He won the whole of the tournament by a mile, but when I bashed out those 12 letters, D-A-V-I-D B-E-C-K-H-A-M, I never imagined he would end up where he is today.

While researching this book, I contacted George Best, who had been at Old Trafford, the home of Manchester United and the venue for the last stage of the Soccer Skills competition that Sunday. He was a spectator at the competition because, after the boys had left the pitch, Manchester United played Spurs in a wonderful, see-sawing game in the old First Division that ended 3–3. Best remembered the match, but could not recall taking much notice of the youngster who had dribbled the ball with such panache and shot with the power we all know now, because, well, would you?

For me it's funny how things go; Bobby Moore and David Beckham linked by a soccer school. It is curious, but that is just the start. Twenty years apart, the two greatest names in English football were brought up in streets 15 minutes away from each other and their careers have made them more globally famous than any other player from Britain. As children, one lived in a house with the number 43, the other 143. Coincidence? Probably. But is the fact that they both came from the same corner of England's capital also a coincidence?

The east end of London is made up of an area that takes in seven boroughs east of the city and those that run through the north side of the River Thames, a busy metropolis of housing and business, leading towards the new sites in Canary Wharf where the tallest building in Europe stands. Heading towards the city on a road called Cheapside is the Church of St Mary-Le-Bow, commonly known as Bow Bells. The church has 12 bells and at the top of each hour, they ring out across London, a mellow tenor tone in 41-3-21 in C, leading to a crescendo of noise. Tradition has it that if you are born within the sound of those bells, you can call yourself a cockney. The name is derived from a sixteenth-century word used to mean an egg that was out of shape, often called a 'cock's egg', first accepted into the *Oxford English Dictionary* in 1521.

In his work of 1617, *Ductor in Linguas*, lexicographer John Minsheu wrote: 'A cockney . . . applied only to one born within the sound of Bow Bell that is in the City of London, a term coming first out of this tale . . . A citizen's son riding with his father in the country asked, when he heard a horse neigh, what the horse did: his father answered "neigh". Riding further, he heard a cock crow and said: "Does the cock neigh, too?'"

One area where the chimes can be heard loud and clear is 1.2 miles away from the church itself, along a couple of roads now crammed with office blocks. In Great Queen Street at Lincoln's Inn Fields, the Freemasons' Tavern used to stand, a building that was demolished in 1931 when it was deemed structurally unsafe. It had been built in 1776 and dedicated to freemasonry, and was used for regular meetings of the type that now take place across the world. It was also used for holding musicals, concerts, recitals and balls, but few more significant occasions took place there than the one on 26 October 1863.

In Britain, football clubs started to emerge in the late 1850s. In 1847, a Factory Act had been passed which gave industrial workers time off on Saturday afternoons. Working men used this free time to launch their own football teams. It was a form of relaxation, relief from the grind of standing behind steaming machinery. In 1878, a group of Lancashire railway workers created Newton Heath, a side that 14 years later became Manchester United, now the most glamorous and biggest team in the world.

As more teams were formed, there was a need for more organisation. Suddenly football was moving from being a game that broke up the monotony of working to a sport that needed a structure whereby competitions could be staged on a regular basis. The problem remained until representatives from clubs in London and the south of England decided to meet in the Freemasons' Tavern to discuss creating a body that would solve the issue of the lack of a suitable organisation. On 26 October 1863, the English Football Association was formed for the purpose of setting a code of rules for the regulation of the game in Britain . . . to the background sound of the Bow Bells, the noise that rings across the capital and has become the embodiment of London.

Flick through the pages of the annual football bible, *Rothmans*, and you will see that of the 92 English clubs in existence today, so many have a player from the east end of London. There are many eastenders in the Scottish League, and even as far west as the North American Leagues in the USA and beyond.

Are the high numbers of players to come out of the east end and its Essex border a mere fluke? I wonder, sitting in Row A, seat 22, B block, at Brisbane Road. Perhaps the upbringing of people who have been nurtured into the game is the same in any area. Could it be that working-class life in the east end of London makes people find an escape route on Sunday mornings on the local football pitch? Or is it simply the presence of Robert Frederick Chelsea Moore rising above every dream every youngster ever had to play the game and reach the level he climbed to, creating one huge family, all striving for the same goal that he achieved?

Beckham has become the footballing ideal for every modern youngster, but Moore's face remains as synonymous with the English game now as it did on that Saturday afternoon of 30 July 1966 when he wiped his hands to clean off the sweat of 120 minutes of incredible football and the turbulent emotions that went with it, before shaking hands with the Queen and lifting the World Cup trophy.

A player with West Ham, the east end's most famous club, Moore was a national hero. London football has never had (and perhaps never will have) a greater day. Moore's teammates from West Ham had scored the goals: Martin Peters, born a goalkick away from the West Ham ground itself, and Geoff Hurst, an adopted eastender, who remains the only player to convert a hat-trick in a World Cup final.

But between the rise of Moore and the pedestal that Beckham now finds himself upon lies an incredible story of a line of players who have transformed the game by coming out of the fields of dreams that lie on the east side of the city. Was it just another coincidence that when Sven-Goran Eriksson became the first foreign manager of the English national team, the first domestic game he watched when he arrived in Britain was at West Ham? Interestingly, the backbone of his World Cup team in Japan last summer was made up of players from that area: Sol Campbell, discovered on a pitch in Stratford; Ashley Cole, nurtured with one of the area's top boys' teams; Teddy Sheringham, a

Walthamstow schoolboy; Rio Ferdinand, developed at West Ham; Trevor Sinclair, fine-tuned at the Hammers; and, of course, Beckham himself.

Since Moore walked up those 39 steps at Wembley to collect the World Cup, the area has been rolling out the stories of footballing prowess at an unstoppable rate, with Terry Venables; the knighting of Alf Ramsey; Clyde Best, the black player who challenged the way the game was perceived in Britain; and Laurie Cunningham, the first black player to be capped by England at any level.

Even now Beckham talks of the inspiration he takes from watching old videos of Moore, the most graceful player ever to wear an England shirt. It is ironic that his iconic status grew even greater in 1970, when England's defence of the World Cup ended with defeat against West Germany in Mexico.

Moore's tackle on Pelé in the match with Brazil is without a doubt one of the finest footballing moments – not a goal, a great move or a controversial incident, but a tackle! It took your breath away: his anticipation, his timing, his majestic ability to halt the progress of the greatest player in the world. It was, simply, Bobby Moore at his best. Few moments encapsulate greater the hold Moore had on the game, and on the nation's imagination. No other interception in a football match springs to mind as vividly as this one.

While Moore and Beckham are the most famous football sons of the east, one area of former wasteland is as synonymous with English football as the players themselves . . . Hackney Marshes.

It is a Sunday morning and I am standing by pitch 29. The view is immense. An ocean of colour lies before me. It is black, white, blue, green, yellow, red, orange, grey. There are stripes, hoops, dots, even dashes and sashes.

A gale is blowing and there is little point looking over even as far as pitch 30 because what lies beyond is indeterminable, almost blinding, a blur of moving colour, as if an artist's palate has been tossed in the air. Twenty-two pairs of legs dart about chasing the one colour that is universal in this vast expanse of turf, the white of the round object on the ground.

On pitch 29, the action has stopped. So strong is the wind on this winter Sunday morning that the ball from this game has found its way north-west onto No. 31.

It means a halt to a fine match between the Boston Arms and Spartan United in the Camden Sunday League. It has been a raw, full-blooded first half.

And there he is, a diamond geezer as they would say in these parts, emerging from the granite of a football game played between two competitive sides. He is a little guy with a receding hairline who stands out from the rest, even without the ball . . . and definitely when it comes to him and he shows his quick turn of pace.

Some of these east-end diamonds sparkle more than others on Sunday mornings. The player I am watching is just a face with no name, but he could easily become one. Players like him are a breed apart. They don't thump the ball, they don't hit and hope, they are the difference between wanting a Sunday run-out and hoping a run-out on a Sunday might, just might, lead to something in the week.

Class has the opportunity to stand out on this 350-acre expanse of grass which houses 85 pitches, the largest single area for football in the world.

It is a fact that more goals are scored from the use of the long-ball game between the hours of 11 a.m. and 12.45 p.m. every Sunday here than anywhere else: I dare anyone to dispute it. Some games are organised properly, while others have to call on a member of each squad to run the line, but most actually have a proper referee, a sight not always seen on park pitches of a Sunday morning.

But while some players hit, others hit and hope that one day they will make it like so many others before them.

Hackney Marshes. A place that has embraced the likes of Beckham, Cunningham, Peters, and even to this day, international players such as Newcastle's Lomana Lua Lua, and an endless list of other footballers who turned their Sunday-morning expeditions into a lifelong association with the game, not just at a peripheral level but at the top. We know where they are now, but how did they get there, why did they reach such heights and how did it all start?

It is not so much a mystery tour as one of enlightenment, a journey through football history that might not answer the question of whether an area can actually create good footballers, but will show that it is more than luck that England's famous east-end players all trod a path on the breeding ground of brilliance.

## 2. My Friend Bobby

ON THE DAY THAT BOBBY MOORE DIED IN FEBRUARY 1993, NOEL Cantwell had chosen to go horse racing. He recalls that he had spoken to his great friend just a few days before and had decided to see him later that week; he remembers how weak Moore had sounded on the telephone, how he had asked whether he was coming down to visit him. But Cantwell had had no inclination that the end was so near.

He was on his way back to his home in Peterborough after the day out when he decided to pop into a hotel to catch up with a few buddies. He went past the reception desk when an employee he knew was quick to say: 'It is very sad about Bobby Moore, isn't it?' Cantwell, in his distinctive Irish burr, replied: 'Yes, but he will be all right, he is a battler.' The man said: 'No, he is dead.' Cantwell swallows deeply and stops for a second. 'I could not believe it,' he says now. 'I had been horse racing and I had not been there to see him, my great friend.'

Cantwell had been close to Moore from the moment the smart, blond teenager had wandered into Upton Park for a training session in the spring of 1954 at the age of 13. As a player, he did not have much pace, he did not have reams of skill, he did not score many goals. But even then, he had a presence, a presence like Cantwell had never seen before and does not expect the game in England to be graced with again.

Cantwell is godfather to Moore's son Dean and when he gathered his emotions after hearing of the death, he rang up Bobby's second wife Stephanie to ask if he could say his own farewell. The English public felt quite rightly that Bobby Moore was part of their lives after leading the country to their one and only victory in the World Cup on that cherished day in July 1966, but he was very much a private, family man. Within hours of his death, his body had been removed from his home and taken to a chapel of rest. It was the way he would have wanted it, and the family knew the commotion and outburst of press attention that would occur once the news was announced to the world.

Stephanie agreed that Cantwell could see Bobby. They met at the station near the chapel in East Putney and in a side street next to the cemetery, he was allowed in to see his great friend for a final time. 'I don't know if anyone else outside of the immediate family saw Bobby in his coffin,' says Cantwell. 'But did we have some times together. The man was a one-off, definitely; I have never seen a footballer like him . . . and I do not think I will ever again.'

Bobby Moore was born on Saturday, 12 April 1941 in the bedroom of his parents' house at 43 Waverley Gardens, a small, unassuming road that lies on the cusp of one of the busiest stretches of links between east London and Essex. Even today the chaos of traffic and roadworks, despite being so close, is not heard from the small street with its 68 houses. There is an air of calm about the place.

June Cooper, Bobby's aunt, stands by the front of No. 20, a terraced house like most on the street, and looks towards the house where Bobby used to live; she can see him now, with his blond hair flowing in the wind, and always with a football. Most days on his way home from school he would pop in to see his aunt and uncle Bill, his father's half-brother. June recalls Bobby was always around their house. 'Bobby loved chips and he would come here after school and I would cook them for him. I don't know why – maybe he would get more here than when he was at home,' she says, laughing. 'It never surprised me that he ended up where he did because he was such a good footballer at school.

'We used to go to watch him at the park nearby when he played for the school; in the first half he would be in the defence, in the second, he would be up front. He was only ten at the time and he was in control of the whole game with what he did on the pitch even then.

'But the one distinguishing feature about Bobby was that he was not flash; he was a genuinely caring young man. His mother and father were quiet people; they kept themselves to themselves and he followed the lead that they had set. They had standards and his mother insisted on one thing: her son's name was Robert, not Bobby.'

His schooling started at Westbury Road Junior in Barking before he went to Tom Hood, a bus ride away in Leyton. Even now the latter is planning a tribute to their greatest son, to ensure that his name, his achievements and what he meant to the whole country will be known to a new generation for whom computer games have replaced football in the street.

But the Bobby Moore effect started long before he arrived at Upton Park. Ken Drury is head teacher at Eastbrook School in Dagenham and, in an interview with the *Ilford Recorder* newspaper, he remembered how Moore's name was well known on the Barking football scene even at the age of ten.

'Bobby was a couple of years younger than me and we lived a few roads apart but I was on the other side of the busy A13 stretch, so even though he lived only 300 yards away, it was quite a distance because the road was so busy. We both went to Westbury Junior and normally when you are two or three years older than other kids at school, you don't know them,' he said.

'Bobby was different because he was so good at football. He played for the school team and I used to go to watch the games. He was not a tall boy, he was stocky, nothing like he became as an adult, this elegant figure on the football field that led his country.

'Always, his parents were on the touchline giving him encouragement, always, of course, calling him Robert.'

Moore was captain of the Barking Primary Schools' side that won the distinguished Crisp Shield in 1952 and with local scouts watching many games in the area, Moore's name cropped up all the time. It was passed on to the famous West Ham scout Wally St Pier and Moore was invited to Upton Park to train with a select group of 30 boys who had been drafted in to work with the professionals twice a week.

Malcolm Allison was the star of the Hammers show at the time. He was an inspirational character who brought charisma to the side from his role as a central defender. Allison progressed to become one of the great managerial characters of the 1970s, '80s and '90s because of his endearing manner and he proved a huge influence at Upton Park, ensuring that the team, under manager Ted Fenton, developed the flowing football that remains their trademark today.

During the close season, Allison would go to special training courses at Lilleshall, where the national sports centre was based, and return with books and notes on different ways of doing things advising the coaching staff of what he learnt and wanting the team to try new ideas.

Each Tuesday and Thursday, either Allison, Cantwell or Phil Woosnam, who progressed to become the club captain, would take the training. They earned £1.15 for their night's work but would go home having achieved satisfaction from what they had seen on the pitch, rather than from what was in their pockets.

West Ham could not buy their way to success. They did not have the financial resources that the larger London teams, such as Arsenal and Chelsea had, and their decision to consolidate a strong base with the best local youngsters around coincided with the new philosophy of the Football Association, who wanted clubs to begin this sort of youth structure. Ironically, without much money, the Hammers were ahead of their time and the famous Academy was born. It is still churning out sensational young talent: Joe Cole, one of the brightest England prospects, is the latest product.

The sessions would take place every Tuesday and Thursday, starting at 6 p.m. and lasting for two-and-a-half hours. Sometimes the youngsters would still be playing when darkness fell, such was their enthusiasm and excitement at being at a professional club and being coached by players who were happy to step in to administrate. If evidence is needed of the top quality the east of London produced, in one group at one time at Upton Park were Moore, Martin Peters, Geoff Hurst and Terry Venables, among others.

West Ham became the 'youth' club of the 1950s, but Chelsea soon hopped onto the bandwagon, and being a bigger set-up, many of the best players moved there, perhaps tempted by the promise of more money.

Cantwell says that Moore stood out at West Ham, and not just for his footballing ability. 'He was an immaculate-looking player even then,' he says. 'Everything . . . was clean, even his shorts and boots.'

They were not all success stories at the Hammers, though. Harry Cripps spent 12 years at Millwall having been turned down by the club for not being 'good enough' while many left football totally after not being taken on.

Along with St Pier, Cantwell, who had joined West Ham in 1952, recommended Moore to Fenton and in August 1956, at the age of 15, he signed amateur terms for the club. The following winter he made his debut for West Ham reserves and then came the moment that changed everything and put his career on the path that took him to 108 England caps, the captaincy of his club, his country, the World Cup and beyond.

Allison had not been his normal self, he had not been playing to the standards he set himself and the club expected; all did not seem right. West Ham were away on a Wednesday night at Sheffield Wednesday and in those days they would stay over in a hotel before returning to London by train the following morning.

That night Cantwell heard Allison coughing through the night, waking up coughing in the morning, and getting up first, still coughing. Cantwell originated from Cork, where there had been outbreaks of tuberculosis after the war; he knew how a person who had the illness sounded and that night in Sheffield, he knew all was not well with his room-mate. When they were waiting on the platform to get the train home, Fenton came up to say that he was worried about Allison, who had not been playing well; the tone in his voice suggested he might even leave him out of the next game.

Cantwell advised Fenton to send Allison for some X-rays. 'I remember his reply, wondering if there was something wrong with his

[Allison's] ankle,' he recalls. 'I said "No, send Malcolm for a chest X-ray."'

The next day, the Friday, Dr Thomas, the club's doctor, sent for Malcolm after the tests had been carried out to tell him that they had shown he had a shadow on his lung. 'Malcolm came out and he was crying,' says Cantwell. 'He put his head on my shoulder, said he has had it and that he thinks he has TB.' Allison had part of his lung removed and Cantwell recalls the day that he went with Moore to see him convalescing in a home in Midhurst in West Sussex.

'We were on the way back in the car and it was announced that the plane carrying the Manchester United team had crashed in Munich; it was 6 February 1958,' he says.

Allison was out for the rest of the season. Cantwell took over the captaincy and West Ham progressed to win the Second Division title, securing their success with a 3–1 triumph at Middlesbrough on the final day to confirm their position at the top of the League.

The following season arrived and Allison worked hard to get fit before the team's first game in the First Division, at home on a Monday night against Manchester United, a side still shattered from the effects of the tragedy just a few months previously, when so many of their team had died.

United had a new forward from Blackpool called Ernie Taylor and Cantwell was called into the manager's office by Fenton. He was asked who he would play at left-half in the game.

'Malcolm Allison was my very best friend at Upton Park,' says Cantwell. 'And I told the manager I would play Bobby. I felt Bobby could handle Taylor – and that became the debut of Bobby Moore.'

Allison found out that Cantwell had influenced the decision. He never played in the First Division after all; in fact, he never played for West Ham again.

If United, whose side included Bobby Charlton and Dennis Viollet, thought they would be in for an easy ride against the division's newcomers, they were wrong. They were beaten 3–2 and Moore hardly left the first team after that.

Taylor had been a partner of Stanley Matthews at Blackpool. He was not very quick, but he ran at defenders and Moore, who had become a professional the previous May, showed great ability in his timing of tackles, ensuring he was the perfect foil. Some people believe this first game for West Ham was one of his best ever.

Ken Brown had stepped into the fold when Allison was first ill, and he was at West Ham for 17 years. No one played alongside Moore more often than the man who progressed to become manager at Norwich, and he recalls what he used to put him through each game.

'Bobby used to give me kittens most of the time,' says Brown. 'He was unique because he had such good control. Every ball that used to come down to Bobby, I used to go behind him because he was never going to whack it, he wanted to use it all the time. It was bred in me to go behind him but he never once missed it, I was there as a stop-gap that never had a gap to stop.'

Terry Neill, the Northern Ireland international who played for and then managed Arsenal, tells an equally captivating story about the respect Moore had for his friends on the pitch.

'Bobby and I grew up together as youngsters in London and at a very early stage, we agreed on a pact,' says Neill. 'We decided that if we were playing against each other, whatever side won a corner, neither of us would go up to intimidate the other. It was a pact we never broke. I miss him now like hell.'

One of Moore's major concerns was his pace, though it did not look like it would be troubling him on one of the many mornings when the West Ham players arrived at their training base in Grange Hill in Essex. They say football has changed with the times, that the vast sums of money involved now have taken the fun out of the game, and when you hear of a story like this one, you realise that is perhaps true.

It was pre-season and the players were being put through their paces with a series of long runs to help them regain their fitness. Fenton was sitting in his car, watching as his squad charged around the country lanes in what had become a regular scenario in the build-up to the season.

The good players were not the great runners, but on this particular day, Moore and the club goalkeeper Ernie Gregory had the lead ahead of Cantwell and John Bond, another famous name who progressed from the side to a distinguished career in management. The players wore roll-neck tops and tracksuit bottoms and by the time they reached one of the steeper climbs, sweat was pouring off them, Moore and Gregory were in front of the other pair, sensing, excitedly, that they were going to be ahead of them at the finish, where Fenton was waiting to greet the quicker runners.

Unbeknown to them, Bond always carried spare change in his pockets. 'We were running along when the bus came by,' says Cantwell. 'Bondy shouts out, "Right, let's jump on it." I said, "We can't." But on we climb and make ourselves unnoticed at the back, and off we go, up the hill and we jump off. At this stage Bobby is looking behind him and we are not even in view, he thinks he has done it. But we are about 500 yards from the finish line.

'We charge first across the line, sprinting home and Ted gets out of his car to congratulate us. Bobby and Ernie arrive and cannot believe what they have seen.

'It was not the only time we did that, but no one told the manager. It was the sort of fun we used to have in what was a tremendous atmosphere.'

Moore's pace, or lack of it, was always a concern to him. Cantwell says: 'He was very serious about his football and you had to be careful not to say the wrong thing. He asked me if you could be a good player if you haven't got pace because that was always his worry.

'He attempted to become faster by running more but if you are slow, you are slow. I told him that Johnny Haynes at Fulham was a marvellous player with tremendous vision, who could read a game wonderfully, but he had no pace. That pleased Bobby: he sensed he could become a good player.

'Bobby was not great in the air but when he came onto the pitch, he pulled his sleeves down and just played. Even when he first started, he was immaculate during games. It was as though he ran out onto the pitch just after his mother had ironed his kit – and at that end, he rarely looked different.

'He had such wonderful anticipation, his passing ability was fantastic along with his knowledge of how to read the game. Somehow he knew things were going to happen before they did and he had a knack of freeing himself . . . from getting into tackles that he did not need to.

'He was like a free player at the back, wonderful passing, good control with his left and right foot and I can never remember Bobby having a scar on his face; he would just leave it to us plebs to get involved in the clashing of heads. He would say, "You get the scars."

'He was never dropped from the team and he never sustained any injuries and I don't think he ever broke anything. What's more, his shorts were never dirty because rarely did Bobby Moore have to make emergency tackles. He was always standing on his feet.

'The theory that it might have been from his days playing in the streets, when you would cut yourself if you dived in, could be correct because he was always standing on his feet. He would never be falling over the place because his tackling would be timed so well.'

Ray Wilson was England's left-back at the World Cup finals in 1966 and he remembers Moore being the colossus at the back whenever they played alongside each other.

'There was no edge to Bobby at all,' says Wilson, who was playing when Moore made his debut for England against Peru when Bobby Robson, now in charge at Newcastle and of course the former England manager, was injured.

He added: 'Once he made it into the side, it was quite obvious that he was going to stay there. He might have been in his early 20s but he was absolutely world class. It was like he was aiming to set his stall out each game to be the best defender at that time.

'He had the character to rise to the special occasion and the higher the stakes, the better he would play.'

Wilson won 68 caps for England and remembers the way Moore used to make the most of the ball, never content to waste a pass or make a clearance for the sake of it, if the ball could be played instead.

'He would use it so well,' said Wilson. 'If I had won the ball in a tackle, he always made himself available, so I would always be free of trouble once I got it. Sometimes he would even knock me off the ball to be in there first to play it away. He was remarkable for a defender in the way he distributed it.'

It was typical of Moore that because he felt he lacked pace, he would turn the game to his advantage.

Cantwell says: 'I always admired the way he would never get too tight on a striker until the ball had been played. He knew he did not have great speed, so Bobby used what he did not have to his advantage. If he was close to the striker and the ball came over the top, he would be beaten in the chase. So before the ball arrived he gave himself five to six yards and then you would not realise how slow he was because of the position he had put himself in.'

Cantwell left to join Manchester United in 1960 and by 1964 Moore had progressed to become captain, leading West Ham to victory in the FA Cup final, the following season in the European Cup-Winners' Cup final and then, in 1966, the ultimate moment for any English football player, leading his country to victory in the World Cup, on the home turf of Wembley with the epic 4–2 defeat of West Germany.

When Cantwell looked on at Moore then, he could sense the presence he had seen in him as a youngster a decade earlier.

'When you think of previous England captains, the longest-reigning one was Billy Wright. He had blond hair and a sense of occasion about him. Bobby did too and he came out of the tunnel with such pride in his build. When Bobby walked out, you could tell his proud manner with the ball under his arm. He was a better captain at Wembley than he was at Upton Park, where it all became a bit too familiar to him. Wembley was him all over.'

Moore had made his international debut against Peru in Lima on 20 May 1962, a game England won 4–0. A year and 9 days later, at the age of just 22 years and 47 days, he took over the captaincy from Jimmy Armfield and the legend was created. England were playing Czechoslovakia away in Bratislava and on the day he became the youngest person to skipper his country, the team won 4–2.

Bobby Moore's early years at West Ham make a mockery of the Ferraris, Mercedes and Bentleys that now pack the car parks of modern-day football clubs. He used to travel from his home in Glenwood Gardens in Ilford by trolley bus to training, meeting up with Allison, who lived not too far away in Barkingside; most days they would arrive together at around 9.45 a.m. and as a youngster Moore always wanted to learn, picking the players' brains about football, tactics and the game in general.

It was a set routine. They would train between 10 a.m. and 12.30 p.m. and then go to a café called Cassataries in the Barking Road near the Upton Park ground, where they would go upstairs and just sit and talk about football for hours. Then a few of the players would go back to Upton Park and train on the pitch in the afternoon. It drove the groundsman crazy, particularly if it was on a Thursday because on the Friday morning he would have to start preparing the pitch again for the match 24 hours later. He would go up to Fenton's office to complain, but the manager was delighted that he had players who trained more than they were asked to. In the end, the groundsman resigned.

Moore never won a League Championship medal, but for three years running he led teams out at Wembley to historic triumphs. In 1964, West Ham beat Preston 3–2 to win the FA Cup, the following year they won the Cup-Winners' Cup by defeating Munich 1860 2–0, and in between Moore was made the footballer of the year before his crowning moment arrived.

He was captain of his country for 90 matches, a record he shared with Wright, and on the afternoon of 30 July 1966, when goals from West Ham teammates Hurst and Peters, led England to World Cup final glory, Moore became the biggest name in football in Britain.

If ever there was an illustration of the effect Moore had at the back, it came in this historic tournament. When Portuguese legend Eusebio scored in the semi-final against England, it was the first goal England had conceded in the whole of the competition.

The team made an indelible mark on the country, but for the people of Ilford, where Bobby lived with Tina, it was strange. They had a superstar on their doorstep but they did not need to knock at his house or congratulate him all the time because although Bobby was the ultimate hero, he did not seek attention.

The domestic season after the 1970 World Cup finals, where England, as defending champions, had reached the quarter-finals but had been beaten by West Germany 3–2, began with the country believing the team had been good enough to have retained the trophy.

It had been a dramatic time for Moore, who was accused of stealing a bracelet when the team were in Bogotá in Columbia during their pre-competition preparation for the finals in Mexico. Football fans need something to seize upon – and when West Ham arrived at Old Trafford for a league game, the Manchester United supporters were waiting. The Stretford End at Old Trafford started singing, 'Where's the bracelet, Bobby Moore? In your handbag?' Out of nowhere, he went up to them and started conducting like he was at the front of a choir leading them in a singing routine that he was enjoying as much as they were. Moore's presence off the pitch, in the way he could read life, was as absorbing as his football was on it.

Barry Fry, the jovial, charismatic manager of Peterborough and one of the most popular characters in the game today, was at the annual Football Writers' Dinner in London when Moore stepped in to save what could have become an embarrassing moment. He had got to know the England captain through his days as a player and then their relationship grew closer in the game. In fact, they both ended being manager of Southend, Moore between 1984 and 1986 and Fry seven years later.

'Bobby was a gentleman on the field and off it. He was fantastic to be with socially; if you spoke to him, he looked you straight in the eye and he took notice of every word you said,' says Fry. 'And he would always put others before himself, which is a wonderful characteristic in a person.

'One night at the football dinner, Bobby was on the top table with George Best. George was a close friend of mine and I asked him how he was. Bob said he was in a state through drink and that it was probably a good idea to get him home.

'Discreetly we took him out and waved down a taxi. Bob gave the driver a score because he felt in that environment, with sportswriters and George in a bad way, that if he had fallen off his chair, he would have been slaughtered. Best was gone before anyone knew anything different. The great vision of Bobby Moore, even off the pitch, showed that he was a terrific leader of men.'

'He could drink with the best of them,' recalls Fry. 'But you never saw him drunk, you never saw him in a state, you always saw him pristine and proper. Bobby Moore had too much respect for himself for something like that; he was a one-off.'

Cantwell and Moore had some great times. He recalls particularly the occasion that Bobby came to the opening of his pub. 'The next morning Bobby rang me to say that he seemed to have misplaced a ring and could I look for it,' says Cantwell, who had been Moore's best man when he married his first wife Tina in 1962. 'We look everywhere, from the ash trays to the dustbins, and we cannot find it.'

Not long after Cantwell became involved in running a night club and Moore again visited on the opening night; he was manager at Southend at the time and was invited to stay.

'Bobby insisted he went home because he had an early start the next day; I told him he could leave us early but he said no. Then the next morning, the telephone goes at 7.30. He had been driving home, all alone on the road, it was a beautiful night with the silvery moon shining when he was stopped by police, breathalysed and found to be over the limit.

'After the ring incident and this driving offence, he said: "Noel, do

me a favour. Next time you open something, do not tell me about it!"
That was Bobby; such fun.'

Time catches up with every player. Moore's last international
appearance came on 14 November 1973 against Italy at Wembley, a
game England lost 1–0.

In the FA Cup third round the following January, Moore suffered
an injury in a match with Hereford and it proved his final game for
the Hammers' first team. He played a reserves match later in the year
and, less than a week later, moved across London to join Fulham.

Twelve months later the FA Cup final was upon the country, West
Ham against Fulham at Wembley, and Moore was playing against the
team that had turned him into one of the game's greatest sons.

It was a one-sided match, West Ham winning 2–0, but even in
defeat, the presence of Moore was too much for one player. Clyde
Best, the Bermudan international, had been in and out of the West
Ham side as the final drew nearer and in the end, Pat Holland was
chosen ahead of him.

Best remained gracious throughout his time at West Ham and it
was typical of him to take the upset of being left out of the FA Cup
final with dignity; typical too was the way he thought of Holland on
that occasion. It was the first London derby in the FA Cup final
since 1967, when Tottenham beat Chelsea 2–1, and Best recalls:
'There was one place in the team between Pat Holland and myself
and if it had been anyone else, then I would have held a grudge
against them.

'But Patsy was such a good mate of mine that I was genuinely
pleased to see him in the team. We were fighting for the same position
and he was chosen ahead of me; I had played in the quarter-final and
I thought I might be in the team but sometimes in life things happen
because they are meant to happen. There was nothing I could do so
what was the point of feeling bad about it?'

But there was another reason why his world did not come crashing
in when the side was named and he was not in it. That reason was
Bobby Moore.

'Wembley is *his* special place because of 1966,' says Best. 'During my career, I would not have wanted to have to come up against the people who were my idols: Bobby fell into that category. I had played against him enough in training matches and it was good fun, but it would not have been right for me to be running towards him and then maybe going around him or something like that at Wembley when he is on the opposite side.

'He was always a hero of mine because he made the game look so simple. Remember, I had come from a system that was totally different to what was going on in England.

'It was an amateur set-up in Bermuda, we would do things off the cuff during games with no pre-planning and then I arrived here where the whole way of the game is more team-orientated. But Bobby was ready to help. He might have been a world-class player but he was not big-headed; he was just a fantastic person to be alongside because he inspired you when you did not even know it was happening to you. Yet to have taken the ball past him – and I am not saying it would have happened because we all know what Bobby was like – would not have sat good with me.'

Next stop for Moore was a move to the North American football league where he joined San Antonio Thunder the following year for a summer spell in the attempted boom time for the sport in that country, returning to Fulham in 1977 before going back to the USA 12 months later.

His career in management, first at non-league Oxford City and then Southend United, came and went. It was amazing that a person who could inspire so much on the pitch never succeeded in this role.

Even in 1980, when I was a schoolboy, Moore's name was so big that there was never a doubt in my mind – 14 years and three World Cups after England had triumphed at Wembley – to attend his soccer school for a week at a venue not too far from my home. Bobby was not there for much of the time because he was travelling around from school to school, but the coaches he brought in must have been instilled with directives to play the game the way he did.

I cannot say I left at the end of that week a better footballer, but what clearly stands out is that each day, however much individual or team practice was taking place, there was so much importance put on making use of the ball properly, particularly when the coaching came to defence.

I always regret not having the chance to ask Moore whether that was one of the aims of the school, teaching people to play the game the way he did, but then I often think it would have been a silly question: how could you teach anyone to play the game the way Bobby Moore did?

The course left me with some great memories, and when Bobby arrived for the closing ceremony, it completed a fantastic week: I shook his hand and we had a quick exchange of words.

I could not wait until the new season started for my Sunday side, because although I had not really learnt any new tricks during my week under the guidance of the Moore way of playing, I felt more confident on how to approach the game. I used to play in goal often, but from that moment on during matches, I would happily collect a back pass with my feet and had no qualms about dribbling out from the edge of the box. So, if the Moore school taught me one thing, it was that as much as talent might be decided at birth, confidence can be gained by listening and absorbing the lessons of someone with a special ability to play the game.

I met him properly only once more after that, when he was in charge at Southend and the interest was growing about his reign. He spoke calmly at the press conference after the match I attended, about how he wanted more out of his side and how he hoped to improve upon results. At the time it always made me wonder – as I still do today – why his teams did not succeed more during his time as a manager.

Moore's words that night were as precise as the way he used to play the game: he did not waste sentences if he did not have to. If his team talks were like this, how could players fail to become inspired? Just his presence in the dressing-room should have been enough to persuade a team to want to succeed for him, as he did when he was at West Ham.

A successful career in management was not to be and he moved into the world of the media to ensure he kept his hand in with the game he loved. He was a journalist reporting for the *Sunday Sport* newspaper in 1989 at Hillsborough when 96 fans died in the Liverpool–Nottingham Forest FA Cup semi-final, but his own tragedy was closing in.

Moore visited Wembley for the final time on Wednesday, 17 February 1993, in his role as an expert summariser for the London radio station Capital Gold as England beat San Marino 6–0. A week later he was dead. He had announced that he was ill, but the news of his death was a shock because, as Cantwell always says, Moore seemed indestructible.

Colleagues recall how Moore went around the press room at Wembley that last evening, shaking hands with friends, knowing that it was unlikely he would see them again – a final memory of a man who will remain in the heart of English football forever. Eastenders have not had a finer footballer than the man they were proud to call their son.

# 3. Tales of the Marshes

THE HISTORY OF HACKNEY MARSHES IS FASCINATING, LIKE
taking a journey with H.G. Wells and his time machine: there have
been many intriguing characters and stories associated with this
famous grassland. It is hard to imagine the history that lies beneath
the football pitches, because today a constant stream of traffic passes
into the heart of London and the noise detracts from the atmosphere
of the place.

Legend has it that in the eighteenth century, Dick Turpin, the most
famous of highwaymen, would often make his way onto the Marshes
and drink in a place called the Beresford's White House. Before him
the Normans used the Marshes as a burial ground and during the
Second World War, the area became known as a place where rubble
and wastage from bomb-damaged properties was taken. Hackney
Marshes became one of the most famous dumping grounds in
London.

The turning point for the game in the east end came in 1947.
Football had actually been played there since the early 1890s, but
never in the organised manner that the local council in Hackney
decided it would be from then on. An investment was made, the
grass was flattened and on this large site, 120 pitches were designed
and with it, a home was created. Leagues were formed and the
Marshes became the place to play, the Wembley of Sunday-morning
football.

I have met many of the footballers who played on the Marshes, and
their stories are so diverse: from the goal posts to the balls and the

abandoned matches, to the memories of those who have progressed and are still progressing.

One of the fast-emerging stars of the Premiership (fast being the operative word) is Lomana Lua Lua, the striker from the Democratic Republic of Congo. He came to London in 1986, when he was five, and was spotted playing on the Marshes by Colchester United 11 years later. He was offered a trial and became a striker. Now he has to become a regular member of the Newcastle side, having moved from the Essex club for £2.5 million in 1990. He is just another name in a long list of players who have seen this hallowed turf of Sunday soccer lead to a future beyond the 90 minutes.

It is easy to understand why the Marshes have become what they are today, simply by taking a look at a map of London. Each and every area has large amounts of grasslands around it, except the east; there is the famous Victoria Park and of course there is Hackney Marshes, but compared to the rest of the capital, the east end is a mass of housing. Street football was commonplace and in the past it was fairly safe because there were not many cars. Nowadays, a game could not take place without constant interruptions to allow vehicles through, but it was different 50 years ago.

The emergence of Hackney Marshes as a football ground became an organised escape from the games in the road. The 120 pitches were packed every Sunday and the 85 that remain are as busy. The landmark has found the area a place in the *Guinness Book of Records* because it is unique for the number of football pitches contained in one place.

Today Hackney Marshes has been used for a variety of football events, including a national five-a-side championship, and the area has also been the location for television adverts featuring, among others, Eric Cantona.

The Marshes symbolised everything about football in east London: raw, hard, no-nonsense toughness and a win-at-all-costs attitude to the game. The local hospital in Homerton has reported that virtually every week they tend to one injury or another resulting from an incident in one of the games, from the expected broken legs to the odd broken jaw.

So what creates a professional footballer? Is it his skill, his power, his passion, his ambition, his attitude, his desire – or the area he comes from? Was the emergence of Hackney Marshes actually responsible for producing footballers because it gave people the chance to express their talent away from the confines of their own streets?

While it might seem like coincidence that so many of the games' top players have emerged from the east London area, including Bobby Moore and David Beckham, there is no doubting the fact that people who are brought up in places that are not as thriving as others often reveal more drive to make it than those from wealthier parts. History backs this up.

The east end has been poor for a long time. In 1889, a Liverpool-born businessman called Charles Booth, whose studies sparked his interest in how areas evolve, produced the world's first poverty map. From 1896 to 1903 he conducted a survey into the way people lived across the whole of London, and concluded that about 30 per cent of the population in the capital were existing at the lowest levels possible. The most densely populated poverty area was the east end itself; in many respects not much has changed in more than a century since Booth's findings. There were high rates of unemployment, juvenile crime, teenage pregnancy, benefit dependency and a very low educational level in schools, and despite the 100 years that have passed, during which time other parts of London have risen and fallen in terms of their socio-economic status, large parts of the east end have not changed at all.

Major developments have taken place: ironically, one of those was New Spitalfields Market, just a decent goalkick away from the Marshes itself, and of course the area of Canary Wharf, moving out of the heart of the east end, which is now one of the most expensive areas to live and rent office space in the capital, with the tallest building in Europe and spectacular views of the River Thames. But the east end itself is still characterised by a large degree of poverty. It was once an area of eastern Jewish immigration, with very poor Jewish immigrants coming from western Poland and eastern Russia. While there has been a massive turnover of population, there has not been a great increase in the number of families.

Given that the prevailing winds are westerly throughout Europe, anywhere to the east of a city centre is generally poor because that is the direction where all the smoke and the fumes go. Consequently, the more affluent families tend to move to the west, and the housing in the east remains at a lower standard.

London is characterised by a massively sub-divided set of property tenures and consequently much of the land in central London was owned in the past by livery companies and big estates in the city. Large-scale landowners could develop property and receive a good return for it, but in the east end, the extent of property ownership was generally limited to one house, one plot, which meant that it was very difficult to make wholesale improvements to the area. The owner could decide to smash down his 'hovel' and build something new, but if he had a property of equally poor standard to his old one on either side of it, he could not receive a decent rent from the new building, so it was not worth it. The tendency was for people not to improve their buildings; it was, a collective problem: unless everyone did, no one would.

Paul Johnson is a professor of economic history at the London School of Economics and he believes areas can have an effect on the way people conduct their lives. He says: 'What we see now with, say, Canary Wharf is that property companies have come in and over 10–15 years they have built up properties by packaging together a whole block and then they redevelop it because that is the only way they can get the return on it.'

With the lack of green areas in the east end, there were not many places for children to spend their leisure time, but most people brought up in the area felt that anyone could kick a ball in the street. George Petchey, the manager of Orient between 1971 and 1976, was raised in Whitechapel and says: 'You have to go back to the Second

World War, even before then. Kids used to play in the roads and street teams were formed. The games were quick, and short, and hard and you battled as well as you could.

'There were no green fields for the eastenders because the schools did not play matches. But then when you ended up playing on a pitch, you thought you were at Wembley. It was wonderful, having grass where you could tackle.

'When I lived in the east end just before the war, there was a great atmosphere. We used to play cricket in the street as well. There were no fears about danger from cars because they did not come down sometimes if they saw you were playing. But there were so few cars anyway.'

Traditionally, sport has been a route of escape from poverty. As the opportunities available to children brought up in deprived areas are so narrow, those who do succeed are more likely to do it through something like football or boxing.

Johnson points out: 'There might be 15 year olds at Eton or Harrow with the same sporting aptitude, but they can say "Do I want to be an astro-physicist or do I want to be a Premier League player, because I am fantastic at maths and I am damn good at football?" They have an option. You have much less likelihood that a similarly gifted person from a more privileged background would take the route of football, because they do have these alternatives and it is likely the kids from poor areas don't.

'It is why football is so much more important for poor kids. It is not just in Britain, the stories from Brazil are the same. There are low expectations from schools and when people do succeed, they stand out.'

Not that every footballer who stood out from the east end actually came from the poorest of the areas, Tower Hamlets, but most that did make it have not forgotten where they came from. You can take a person out of the east end, but can you take the east end out of the person?

Take David Webb, the battling, at times ferocious centre-half who made his name playing for Chelsea. He lived in Stratford, about 30 minutes from Hackney Marshes, 30 minutes, that is, if you have to walk it, as he did regularly to meet his 'friends' when they gathered on the famous turf to play football. Not organised games, just a kick-around during the week. He was the one who supplied the ball and he recalls: 'Because I had the function for the means to the game, it would seem that people would want to be my best friend; let's have a game, can we play? These were questions I was asked often, sometimes by people I had never met before.

'We used to have some great games and then once it was over, they would all jump on their bikes and cycle off home, leaving me to walk back the 30 minutes alone. Had it not been for me they would have no game, and when the game was over, they did not want to know me. Football was the link for us all.'

Webb's most famous moment came when he scored the goal that won Chelsea the FA Cup in a famous replay with Leeds at Old Trafford in 1970, a header, with him climbing above Jack Charlton, a World Cup winner four years earlier, to bury the ball in the back of the net for a 2–1 triumph. Twenty-two years later Webb was back at Stamford Bridge as Chelsea's manager at a time when the redevelopment of the ground was starting to take place – the ground now even has its own hotel. Stamford Bridge remains one of the trendiest parts of London, with more wine bars than people, more sushi restaurants than backstreet cafes.

Once he had settled in, Webb called a press conference for some of his closest friends in the media world and decided to take them out to lunch. The venue? A pie-and-eel shop on the Wandsworth Bridge Road. 'What you see is what you get with me,' says Webb, born in Stratford in 1946, and never to forget his roots.

His career started at Leyton Orient, under the managerial reign of Dick Graham, and training used to take place on the Marshes, near their ground at Brisbane Road. 'There were fumes coming out of power stations nearby and we would be running around there to get fit,' he said. 'When you think now of the business made of the healthy way footballers are asked to prepare and train, and then think back to what we must have breathed in during those times, it is unbelievable how the game has changed from us then on the Marshes.'

Twice Webb managed Southend. Ironically Moore did too, and so did Barry Fry, one of the greatest characters in the game today. While he was not from the east end, it was there that his now-famous managerial skills were honed, also by Dick Graham.

Fry had been a schoolboy at Manchester United. He then went to Bolton and after a spell at non-league Gravesend, he joined Orient.

'One day we found ourselves without a trainer, as we used to call it then. As I had been in and out of the team, Dick came into the dressing-room and asked if I would like to have a go,' recalls Fry. 'So I would run on the field, whack a sponge on the injury that the player was complaining about, tell him in my own lovely language to get the hell up and start playing again. Nowadays, we must have doctors and qualified people to attend these players on the pitch; then we had me. Need I say any more?'

Fry was in early one morning at Brisbane Road when the telephone rang. It was Graham; he was tied up and would be late for training. He wanted to know if Barry could take it.

'That was my first experience on the managerial ladder,' he recalls. 'At Orient, in east London, and I had gone from player to sponge man to coach, all in one fell swoop.

'Dick later told me that he saw something in me, in the way I used to gee up the lads. He saw I had a good way of motivating them. I had been thrown in at the deep end. I was out there telling players such as Brian Whitehouse and Cliff Holton, who used to play for Arsenal and Watford, what to do. He was clever, old Dick. Another day he rang in and told me that he was going to be late and could I take charge – "But I want them to have a hard session."

'We trained on the pitch that day and as I am doing this and that with the squad, I look over to the stand where, half hiding from me, Dick was there checking up on me.

'Of course that would not happen today because football was more fun then. There was not the pressure that comes with the game now. Can you imagine a manager being late at all? Then, can you imagine him ringing up his club and the first person who answers the telephone is given the job of taking training.

'We were no less professional but the whole attitude was different. It was important to win but the financial implications were not there.

'But I don't blame the players because that is the way football has gone in the marketplace and if you are told you are going to be offered £50,000 a week by your boss to stay in your job, what are you going to do? Say no? Of course you are not, but what it has done is take away that fun feeling because every game can mean so much.'

Fry, who had been at Birmingham and is now manager of Second Division Peterborough, adds: 'But what always makes me laugh more than anything is the way the pre-game diets have now changed. Today, it is all pasta, chicken, everything good for a certain few hours before a game.

'Then, it was steak, egg and chips washed down with a brown ale at 11 a.m., play the game and on the way home, fish and chips in the coach. You still had to entertain during the game, and it still hurt you if you lost, but it was just a game.

'And with all these special diets, different ways of training, warm-ups, warm-downs, there are more injuries now in the game than we ever had.

'I love being a manager and I have Dick Graham to thank for it; the east end of London certainly played the key part in my career. What would I do without football, I could not tell you, but I do know that if my path had not started in the east end it may never have begun at all because life can be like that.

'Dick taught me some great things and I remember when I first took charge at Dunstable, we needed to raise some money for the club and the players had not been paid. I rang George Best up, we had been together at Manchester United and were friends and I asked him if he would bring a team over. It turned into such a huge night that it was even reported on *News at Ten*, all the national newspapers were there and the club made enough money to pay the players.

'Be clever, don't be afraid to ask and throw yourself in the deep end because if you try, you cannot ask more of yourself: a bit like Dick did when he gave me the chance because you never know if you don't try and it has led to me having a great time in the game.'

Harry Redknapp, who made his name at West Ham both as a player and a manager, used to go to watch his father play on Hackney Marshes as a boy. He remembers one game very clearly, or 20 minutes of a game anyway.

'Whatever pitch you were given at the Marshes, you just hoped it was not one of those near the river [the River Lea],' he says. 'My dad's team were unlucky on this particular day.

'The game kicked off and it was particularly windy and after about ten minutes, the ball ends up in the river and it has gone. The current is so strong that there is no point chasing it but you can imagine the scene with half-a-dozen of them trying to. The opposition bring out their ball and not long after it, the same thing happens. The outcome: no balls, no game, match abandoned.'

The Marshes was Sunday football at its raw best; there was no elegance about the place, just a stack of pitches and a stack of games. In fact, there were not even any changing-rooms.

Redknapp progressed from spectator to player and he recalls: 'We would come off the pitch on some freezing morning, caked in mud and the only place you could wash off your boots, or yourself, was in the water from the cattle grids. You never thought what had actually passed over there first because you were in such a state. When I look back now it is amazing but at the time no one cared, it was part of what we expected on a Sunday morning and you just got on with it.

'You cannot imagine what it was like with the amount of people all over there together at the same time, cleaning their boots, filthy dirty, mud flying everywhere, as the matches were ending. But that was what Sunday football on the Marshes was all about.'

Even when Redknapp went 'upmarket' it was the same: 'When I

used to play matches in Regent's Park it was no different; there we used to get changed underneath the trees.'

Petchey, who used to go to watch players at the Marshes during his time at Orient, adds: 'I was always disappointed with the way they ran it. The pitches were all full, there would be absolute chaos, balls bouncing from one pitch to another, stoppages and the ball going in the wrong direction. In the end I used to say, "I am not coming here anymore."'

Though he was not discovered there, Petchey brought Glenn Roeder, the current West Ham manager, to Orient and he too has some unforgettable memories of the Marshes. The pitches there were so close together that confusion often reigned about, firstly, whether the ball had gone into the goal and, secondly, whether it was in the right goal or on the pitch nearby, because there were no nets.

Roeder, who was not born in the east end, but in nearby Woodford in Essex, says: 'The organisers ended up leaving the front of the goals white and painting the back of the posts green, so at least you knew where you were shooting.'

I can understand the confusion. The times I went to see games in researching this book, I had to cross one corner of a pitch to get to another and one Sunday morning, I received a wild volley of abuse because I had walked past a ball that had rolled behind me and just left it; the team from the pitch to my left were cursing me for not kicking it back to them, but I had thought it had come from the pitch on the right.

The number of pitches was reduced to 85 when the area was redesigned, but there is still not much room between one touchline and the next. And how many times does a player stop on hearing the referee's whistle only to find that it has come from the neighbouring game? It is something the players have to get used to, but it is all part of their development, as Roeder found. He made his name with Orient as an elegant centre-half, who had fabulous control of the ball and was renowned for the way he would turn defence into attack with a counter-attack all of his own.

Roeder moved to QPR after helping Orient reach the 1978 FA Cup semi-final, where he was captain of Terry Venables' team, before leaving London for Newcastle and then going into the coaching and managerial side of the game. He was part of the England coaching squad that reached the 1998 World Cup finals in France under the management of Glenn Hoddle, and in his first season at West Ham in 2001–02, when he replaced Redknapp, he took them to seventh in the Premiership, when many doubted he would last the full term.

He is an astute observer of the game, one of the east end's finest footballing sons from his days at Orient and impressive time at West Ham, and his assessment of the quality of players who come from the region is staggering.

'It is the strongest area of talent in the whole country,' says Roeder. 'There is the route, through from the east end and into Basildon in Essex, where the amount of young talent is immense. The past has proved it and the future is no different. I would take any team on in any part of this country with boys from this area, and that includes places such as the North East, Manchester and Scotland.

'The area is a real hotbed for football. It has been like it down the years because there is such a love of it here and, whatever people think, football is still the working man's sport. And because so many play it, the standards grow and with better standards, you have better quality, which in turn leads to a better foundation.'

What more could the east end want? It may have been poverty-stricken, but it climbed from despair to the heights of the game with the ultimate success achieved by Bobby Moore and his glory boys at the World Cup finals in 1966 . . .

# 4. Wembley Calls

CONTRARY TO POPULAR BELIEF, ENGLAND'S VICTORY IN THE
World Cup final in 1966 was not solely down to the east end, though
Geoff Hurst, who scored a hat-trick, Martin Peters, who converted
the other goal, and captain Bobby Moore all happened to play for the
area's main club, West Ham. Manager Sir Alf Ramsey came from
nearby Dagenham, and the player who left Wembley with more mixed
emotions than any, Jimmy Greaves, was born in East Ham. It remains
one of the great football connections: that three players, Moore, Hurst
and Peters, all came from the same club and transferred their skills in
the domestic game to a level where no England player has matched
them since.

Hurst remains the record goalscorer in West Ham's history. His 252
strikes in 502 matches, during a career spanning 12 years from 1960,
included the period where he set a World Cup record: no other player
has scored a hat-trick in a World Cup final. Though Hurst originated
from Ashton-Under-Lyne in Lancashire, he had little trouble
becoming an 'adopted' eastender.

For Peters, the east end means one thing: the time he spent living
with his grandmother in the house where he was born at 15 Egham
Road in Plaistow, not too far from the Hammers' ground and even
closer to the sport that sent his pulse racing. Jack Young was the first
hero to catch the attention of Peters, who, like most schoolboys,
played football. He soon extended his interests to another event:
speedway.

Young was Australian, and in 1951 and 1952 he was the world

champion. Young won those world titles at Wembley – ironic considering what Peters would achieve in the next decade at the same stadium – and the sport was as popular as it has ever been in that era.

Peters was born on 8 November 1943 and he and his parents lived with his grandmother in a house that was just around the corner from the West Ham speedway stadium. His Nana Peters used to take him to watch the racing and then, after the family moved out to Dagenham, he would stay with her during the summer holidays and they would go to the track.

'It was something that I really loved doing,' he says. 'I used to spend two to three weeks in the east end of London with her and going over to the speedway again was fantastic. Jack Young was the star and he was so exciting to watch.'

By the time he was nine Peters had started playing football at a nearby park. He enjoyed cricket too, and he believes that the fact he took the professional route into soccer is due to his wide range of interest in sport; it was so much part of his life and that was the way he wanted it to stay. 'It was not just football with me and when you look at Bobby and Geoff, it was the same. They were both pretty adept at playing cricket; I was okay but not at their level,' he says. 'But sport was something that you latched onto as a kid, it was the best thing to become involved with.'

He attended a school called Fanshaw when he was six, going all the way through from the infant ranks to senior in his time there, nine years altogether, and enjoying playing football in games lessons with a teacher called Archie Hooper. 'He took us when I first started, it was great fun. I stayed in touch but unfortunately, he died last year,' said Peters.

The young player showed signs of promise as a midfielder with intelligence and fine touches. When he joined the England set-up he made a wonderful impression, so much so that manager Ramsey famously insisted he was 'ten years ahead of his time' because he had such vision.

In Dagenham, the Peters' family home was opposite Park Road

Park. 'It was a cornfield which was turned into a massive park,' he said. 'We used to spend hours over there; it was fantastic. Morning, noon and night we would be there. It was 50 yards from where I lived and it was a wonderful place to play football, among other sports.'

He progressed through the school football system and when he was 12, he played for Dagenham boys. He was a member of not only the Under-13s team, but also the Under-15s.

As a schoolboy he played against Terry Venables, and Peters caught the eye of the West Ham scouts. He was invited to the club, where he became part of the academy and progressed to play in every position, even in goal on one occasion.

While the south comes close in terms of quality, the Hackney Marsh connection gives the east an edge, and the amount of players who have come from there to have made an indelible mark on how the game is played and perceived is huge. To this day, and particularly in World Cup years, the English boys of the summer of 1966 are often brought back together to talk about their triumphs: they remain as great heroes today as they were then.

Peters is an MBE now. His career kept him at West Ham between 1962 and 1970, but he did not emerge onto the England scene for the 1966 World Cup finals until the last minute. He made an impact in a friendly game against Yugoslavia on 4 May at Wembley, and impressed Ramsey so much that he selected him for the main event two months later. With 12 minutes left of the final, he scored what looked set to be the winner before Germany equalised and took the game into extra time.

Then Hurst made his way into the record books; it does not get any better, three goals in the World Cup final. Many have tried but failed. In the last two finals, Zinedine Zidane of France and Ronaldo of Brazil have both scored two, but no one has been able to match the feat of Hurst.

Hurst joined West Ham in 1960 and the 12 years he spent there brought glory, 411 league goals, 91 in the cup and the combination of Moore and Hurst provided backbone to the England team.

At West Ham, they won the FA Cup in 1964 at Wembley. Peters did not play in that game, but he was back a year later when they won the European Cup-Winners' Cup and took their first steps towards the World Cup.

A footballer's life, the way you are looked upon for the rest of your time as a player and whether you are included when they start to talk about legends, can all depend on fate.

Jimmy Greaves scored 44 times for England after making his debut away to Peru in 1959, when he found the back of the net twice. He is the country's third-highest goalscorer behind Bobby Charlton (with 49) and Gary Lineker (48), but his greatest chance to show his skill on the largest stage and to the widest audience was denied him.

Greaves was a Spurs supporter even though it would have been much easier for him to go to West Ham from where he lived in East Ham, and he seemed destined to play for Tottenham, such was the aspiring talent of this goalscorer supreme. But he joined Chelsea, then had a disappointing spell at AC Milan before landing at Spurs under Bill Nicholson in 1961, and setting off on a scoring run that made him an England regular. On his debut in a reserve game he scored with a hat-trick – typical Greaves.

This son of the east end could not stop scoring, but his chances of playing in the World Cup finals looked to be disappearing when he was diagnosed as suffering from Hepatitis B in 1965, an illness that kept him out of the game.

Greaves came back in the only way he knew, scoring goals and looking to make up for lost time. He made the squad for the finals and played in the group games, but sustained an injury before the quarter-final match with Argentina. Hurst replaced him and scored the winning goal, and Greaves did not play again in those finals. It was a turning point if ever there was one for this east-end striker.

Another member of that 1966 World Cup-winning team, Yorkshireman Ray Wilson, looks back on how the ever-changing picture of the England team altered with this linchpin of players from the east end. Wilson played with, and against, Greaves, and remains to this day impressed by his ability to score what he believes are the toughest goals – those when you have only the goalkeeper to beat.

'He would make the keeper do all the work and there is such an art in that,' says Wilson. 'When I think how I would feel charging through on goal . . . but Jimmy was so casual in the way he did it. He was like lightning onto anything, he was so difficult for defenders to handle and he had this ability to see things in the game before the defenders.

'The only player I have seen since then with the capability of doing it as well as Jimmy used to is Michael Owen.

'But I reckon that the majority of Jimmy's goals were scored from ten yards or less, because he had such instinct. If the ball came to him in those positions, he rarely failed. It was a tough decision for Alf to make to pick Geoff, but he was brave once he had made it and look at the way it turned out.

'Jimmy was pretty low and he has had to stick with all the what-might-have-beens over the years, every time the game is shown on television and particularly around World Cup occasions when 1966 becomes a focus again. It is funny the way things go: if we had not won the Cup in 1966, it would have just been passed by.'

When Hurst came into the team there was shock at Wembley that he kept his place for the final ahead of Greaves, as Ramsey stayed with the formula of Roger Hunt of Liverpool and him. Peters and Hurst, the two boys from the east end's top team, had to fit in very quickly to an England set-up that was destined to win the trophy for what remains its one and only time.

Wilson says: 'Martin fitted in no problem and he went on to show he was world-class. You do not win as many caps as he did if you were not of the quality he was.

'The effect of Geoff was quite amazing. As we were the home side, every team we played did all they could to try to defend against us, fending off everything we did.'

In that opening phase of group matches, England drew 0–0

with Uruguay in their first game, before goals from Hunt helped them beat Mexico and France. Greaves did not find the net and, against the French, he suffered a leg injury that opened the way for Hurst.

'Geoff gave us an option when he came into the side,' said Wilson. 'If we were struggling, he would be able to put the pressure on the opponents' defence with his ability to get the high balls. And he was not just a burly centre-forward who was knocking people about everywhere. He was a shrewd footballer, good on the ball, and he did the trick to take us into the semi-finals.'

The final itself is perhaps the most well-known piece of English sporting film, with West Germany taking the lead through Helmut Haller before Hurst equalises, Peters scores in the 78th minute and then Weber scrambles home a last-minute leveller to take the game into extra-time; Hurst's time, with the controversial goal against the crossbar and then the famous last-gasp fourth.

It has been seen so many times, with its famous commentary, but what was it like for the players who were watching as the West Ham centre-forward sent England into the record books?

'I can see that goal going in now,' says Wilson, the left-back that day. 'But what always staggers me, and it did so at the time, was that there were so few players in the German half. It looked like everyone had gone home.

'They had to throw everyone forward and while it looked like a simple goal, he took it so well.

'I was thinking about Geoff while watching this year's World Cup final as Ronaldo scored twice. I remember four years earlier seeing Zidane and thinking "Geoff still holds the record . . . just." I bet he was sitting thinking that it might go. And now he has it for another four years.'

Let the party begin. Moore collected the cup, and Wembley had never known a day like it. Moore, the captain, was made the Player of the Tournament and when Peters talks about the final, he reflects that much as he would have loved to have scored the winner, it was more his annoyance that England allowed the game to slip away so near to the end that stands out.

Ramsey, who had been manager of Ipswich from 1955–63, leading them to the First Division championship in the 1961–62 season, had achieved the ultimate. A man who insisted on his privacy, he had put together a squad that he ensured would gel, on and off the pitch.

Wilson remembers: 'There was such great camaraderie, the company between us all was fantastic. There were few players who would get into Alf's squad who were not good mixers. That was important to him. I am sure he actually brought people into the squad for one match just to look at them and feel them out, to see how they fit. If they did not seem the part, then they might not be back again.

'Nobody teamed up in pairs or in threes – you would not sit in the same seat at dinner in the hotel all the time or with the same people. I am sure Alf set out to do this to make sure we all got on, so he could tell whether we were going to all pull together. A great bit of management because it worked.'

Wilson played for both Huddersfield and Everton and he remembers how much he used to enjoy heading down for matches in the east end at West Ham.

'The lovely thing about it was that they always wanted to play football and it is a tradition that has gone on right until this day,' he says. 'You always knew you were going to be in for a good game because they did not sit back, they did not play negative, they just tried to entertain their way to victory.

'But it is interesting that they never had great sucess in the League in all that time, even with Bobby, Geoff and Martin, the players who were so influential in the World Cup. Though they won domestic and European cups, I was reading that they always had just an average league position. Strange how things like that happen.

'But there was something fashionable about West Ham, they knew they had some special players. Not that you could tell because they were straightforward guys; they never changed.'

So, just what was it like to be a supporter from east London, at

Wembley that day, watching your neighbours win the World Cup?

Ian Cole is the former chairman of the Sports Writers' Association of Great Britian. In 1966, at the age of 19, he was on the terraces at Wembley and if World Cup 2002 brought car horns and flags galore, it was not quite like that then. This is his fascinating story of the finals, a viewpoint rarely seen – that of the fan.

Uncle Frank had a dog called Trixie. She was a very ordinary mongrel, but she was West Ham through and through. Twice in her recent memory she had been dressed in claret-and-blue coat, ribbons, scarf and rosette and twice her master had returned from Wembley shouting about Hammers and Irons and singing a song about Bubbles.

This time was different. Trixie was kitted out in red, white and blue. Her rosette bore the name 'England' and while her master still talked endlessly about that nice Mr Moore, there were people called Banks, Charlton and Stiles as well.

It was 30 July 1966, World Cup final day, and Trixie's role was to wag her tail encouragingly as Frank set off for the game and bark in approval upon his return. It had worked for the opening game of the tournament three weeks earlier – well, at least England didn't lose! – so superstition dictated that Trixie should behave in like manner for each subsequent match.

Scenes just like that were possibly being acted out across the land, not that you would know about it. For while there was a buzz of excitement as England made their tentative progress, the country was still more than 30 years away from Beckham-mania. There was plenty of bunting in the streets, but the flag was the Union Jack rather than the cross of St George. High streets were deserted for the England games but there was no point crowding into a pub and making a lot of noise in 2002 fashion because very few pubs had televisions. So people invited their friends home to gather round their 14-inch black-and-white sets.

My best friend at the time, one David Lambert, watched the final at Old Parkonians Sports Club in Glenwood Gardens, Ilford. To get to the clubhouse you went down an alleyway between a row of typical semi-detached suburban houses. One of these sported a floral rosette on the front door, with the inscription 'Good Luck England'. The residence was that of Bobby Moore, captain of England, and his wife Tina; nothing Posh about our Bobby. No Beckingham Palace for this celebrity couple, though they were soon to move to the relative opulence of Chigwell.

Uncle Frank and I had done our homework earlier in the season, filled in the coupon in the national press and sent off our postal orders. We had a season ticket to every game in England's group – five at Wembley, one at White City, plus quarter-final, semi-final and final.

Wembley's 100,000 capacity was more than half standing, so we stood behind the goal in the same bay, more or less in the same spot, for every game. The bizarre detour to White City came on a rainy Friday night and featured France v. Uruguay. White City was a dog track and a premier athletics stadium that had seen memorable races between Zatopek and Kuts, Bannister, Chataway and Ibbotson. Queens Park Rangers played there from time to time, but never in front of the 45,000-sized crowd that gathered that evening. Every England game was a sell-out and the noise was deafening, while the group games featuring France, Mexico and Uruguay were less well attended.

Connoisseurs of the game, among whom Uncle Frank and I placed ourselves, would offer polite applause from time to time. Ritual and superstition played a part in our World Cup adventure. Frank and I met before every game at Marylebone Station, a venue more renowned for its position on a Monopoly board than for the reliability of its train services. Marylebone, just around the corner from Baker Street, was a throw-back to the Sherlock Holmes era and was pressed into service to relieve the crush on the Metropolitan Line to Wembley Park. A special halt, just a single platform, was opened at the tunnel end at Wembley, which suited us because that was the end our tickets were for.

World Cup final day produced typical July weather, sunshine and heavy showers. We were at the stadium in good time and asked someone to take a picture of the pair of us, festooned in our colours, outside the entrance to Block D. We wore our England rosettes, caps and scarves with pride and carried flags.

Rosettes were popular fan accessories and I had decided to buy a rosette of each of England's opponents, starting with the light-blue and black of Uruguay, the green of Mexico, and the blue of France. I mounted each one on a board, which I hung on my bedroom wall. Underneath each rosette I wrote the result and scorers. I remember rather sheepishly approaching a seller to buy the final piece of my personal souvenir – a black, red and gold rosette of West Germany. I quickly hid the rosette in a bag.

There was a special programme for the final. I had bought the souvenir brochure for the whole tournament, diligently filling in the scores along the way. I chuckled at Italy 0 North Korea 1 and couldn't wait to see the TV highlights. Obviously, if you were at a game you sometimes missed some of the others, so it was some days before I caught up with Pak Doo-Ik's stunning winner.

Her Majesty Queen Elizabeth was paying her second visit to the World Cup on final day. She had opened the tournament on a Monday night 19 days earlier, after an opening ceremony which consisted of children marching around Wembley's running track behind a board bearing the name of each competing nation. No fireworks, no dragons, no razzmatazz. A military band played songs from the West End shows; it was all very English.

Young success: Bobby Moore holds aloft the Barking Primary Schools Championship Shield (Picture: *Ilford Recorder*)

Radio Hammers: The West Ham players listen to the FA Cup draw. (From l–r) Harry Redknapp, Bobby Ferguson (front), Bobby Howe, Billy Bonds, Frank Lampard Snr, Martin Peters and Geoff Hurst
(Steve Bacon/*Ilford Recorder*)

ABOVE: Heading for goal: Clyde Best in typical scoring form
(Steve Bacon/*Ilford Recorder*)

ragic: Laurie Cunningham, one of Orient's greatest players (Colorsport)

# Dynamic David steals the Old Trafford show

**By Richard Lewis in Manchester**

CHINGFORD schoolboy David Beckham broke all records to become the 1986 TSB Bobby Charlton Soccer Skills champion in Manchester on Sunday.

Against all the odds David produced the performance of his life to capture this prestigious title ahead of competitors upto six years his senior.

David (11½), a striker with crack local club Ridgeway Rovers, demonstrated his amazing football versatility by winning all five of the gruelling tests that make up the skills championship.

And reward for his victory is a special training holiday to Europe next year — probably to Barcelona.

Multi-talented David was the single star of the show and produced real top form in the five categories — ball juggling, target shooting, short passing, dribbling and long passing.

And it was the latter two of the five that gave him the most joy for they were staged on the pitch at Old Trafford, the mighty home of Manchester United, prior to the start of their big LIVE televised match with Tot-

tenham in which champion he stood out among them all."

This tremendous triumph brings to an end months of training for David who reached these finals after winning a qualifying tournament on one of the summer schools run by Bobby Charlton.

David's parents, Ted and Sandra, were in Manchester with him for this special weekend and his father said: "This was the second year that David went on the course.

## Reward

"It was during the summer holidays, only for a week, but now it has brought such great rewards."

It's to no surprise that David, a right winger with the Ridgeway under-12s, has ambitions of becoming a professional player. And this is as good a base as any to build on.

Last year's champion of the skills competition was Vietnamese boy Hung Wang, who was immediately picked for the select squad at the Li-

chance of learning valuable techniques from the stars of today.

David is such an example. When he was on his course in the summer, he was able to learn a variation of different skills from Charlton himself and also the chance of meeting and learning from his great idol Robson.

Ted Horton, Head of the Business Development for the local TSB area, said: "We really have made a great success out of these schools.

"And we've had such great co-operation from Bobby Charlton himself. He spends so much time with the kids and is such a magnificent influence. We can't speak more highly of him."

David's example is proven success for these great summer schools and his brilliant skills are rubbing off with his performances with Ridgeway.

It's a great honour for the local area and fitting that David should be shooting his way to personal success on a day when his club Ridgeway scored their 1000th goal since their formation four and a half years ago.

Together they make quite a team!

BRILLIANT David Beckham, pictured with proud parents Sandra and Ted after his superb triumph at Old Trafford on Sunday. He fought off nerves to win the TSB Bobby Charlton Soccer Skills Final in real style. (1045)

**Glory days: how Beckham's victory was reported in the pages of the *Chingford Guardian (Newsquest London/Guardian)***

| Gp.12 MIKE MADDEN | **Score Chart** | WEST GERMANY ⑫ | | | | |
|---|---|---|---|---|---|---|
| 1986 11yrs. Name | AGE | Long & Lofted Passing | Dribbling | Target Shooting | Touch/Juggling | Short Passing | Total Score |
| DAMIAN BARLOW | 11 | | | | | | |
| ROBERT BALL | | | | | | | |
| JOHN BRAWER | | . | | | | | |
| TIMOTHY CWRYNE | | | | | | | |
| RICHARD LAYSSENS | | | | | | | |
| ROY CARUS | | | | | | | |
| ROB. GALLACHAR | | Abs | | | | | |
| ADAM SHAM | | | | | | | |
| ANTONY PATRIMAN | | | | | | | |
| MICHAEL CARPENTER | | | | | | | |
| PAUL PRESCOTT | | | | | | | |
| JON HUMBLE | | | . | | | | |
| HACTOR RWA-PALACIO | | | | | | | |
| RICHARD PARKER | | | | | | | |
| DAVID BRECKNAM | | | | | | | |
| THOMAS ILES | | | | | | | |

David Beckham might be the most well-known footballer in the world, but when he was at the Bobby Charlton Soccer School, the organisers did not even spell his name properly, as this register shows

Chingford soccer sensation signs for the reds

# ☆ DYNAMIC DAVID JOINS UNITED

CHINGFORD football sensation David Beckham has been handed a chance in a million to fulfill his lifetime dream. Ever since the day he first kicked a football he has supported the mighty Manchester United. And on his 14th birthday they signed him up.

What's more David of Hampton Road was...

ABOVE: He's ours: Beckham signs for Manchester United (*Newsquest London/Guardian*).

LEFT: England's Chingford heroes: David Beckham and Teddy Sheringham (Colorsport)

Dugout patrol: Harry Redknapp during his days as Manager of West Ham
(Steve Bacon/*Ilford Recorder*)

East London welcome: England manager Sven-Goran Eriksson (right) at
his first match in England with assistant Tord Grip – at West Ham
(Steve Bacon/*Ilford Recorder*)

East London link: Sol Campbell of Arsenal and Lee Bowyer of Leeds, who both originate from the area, challenge for the ball (Colorsport)

Thought for the day: David Beckham has become the biggest name in football across the world (Steve Bacon/*Ilford Recorder*)

I had been in a 100,000 crowd at Wembley before (for the 1958 Amateur Cup final between Ilford and Woking), but nothing like this. The noise was deafening as Bobby Moore and Uwe Seeler led out their teams. A sizeable German contingent, with klaxons and bells, added to the din.

The three group games had been relatively sedate affairs, enlivened by a crackerjack of a goal against Mexico by Bobby Charlton. It was Alf Ramsey's 'animals' – the Argentinians of Antonio Rattin, with their quarter-final dirty trickery – which really united England's home crowd into a formidable force. We even had a song to greet the Portuguese with in the semi-final: 'We all agree, Banks is better than Yashin; Hurst is better than Eusebio and Portugal's in for a thrashin'.'

The final was tense for us fans. England went behind to Haller, but a real West Ham free-kick – Moore's chip on to Hurst's head – levelled before half-time. Relief at last. Peters puts England ahead. We're only going to win it. Keep 'em out Banksie! But no – oh no! Handball ref! Weber equalises in injury time. It was handball.

Ramsey comes out and administers a pick-me-up and we're off into extra time. Goal! Hurst again, in off the bar. Course, it was a goal. Thank God, the linesman's on our side.

We've won, we've won. Blow the whistle, ref, blow it. It's four. Hurst's hat-trick. Now we really have won it. How we cheered – and cried. Because we were there we didn't notice some of the enduring images of the aftermath: Moore wiping his hands on the baize of the royal box before receiving the Jules Rimet Trophy from the Queen; Ramsey sitting impassively on the bench; Stiles cavorting around the pitch, all gap-toothed and spindly-legged.

We stayed for ages and hugged those around us, cheering and singing until we were hoarse. Then it was off to join the melee for the cattle truck back to London. There were celebrations in the streets, they danced in the fountains of

Trafalgar Square and crowds gathered outside the Royal Garden Hotel in Kensington, where the England team were staying. But in truth the festivities were tame compared with what you would expect if England had brought the World Cup home from Japan.

The World Cup had not yet become a massive media event. There was none of the wall-to-wall overkill that is a feature of modern tournaments. On the Monday after England's victory, the coverage in the *Daily Express* consisted of a front-page story and picture, back-page lead and inside-page lead. Imagine the forests that would be destroyed to accommodate today's supplements and pull-outs!

England, as a nation, went back to work or packed their cases for their fortnight in Blackpool or Margate. The players were allowed a few days off before reporting back to their clubs, for it was already August and a new season was upon us.

As a 19 year old travelling to that game I never fully appreciated that I was witnessing an event that would still be dissected more than 36 years later. So many questions, so many imponderables. What if, for instance, Jack Charlton had not fouled Held to give away Germany's injury-time equaliser? What if the handball had been spotted? Martin Peters, not Geoff Hurst, would have won the World Cup for England. There would have been no extra-time, no over-the-line goal dispute. What if the German defender, seeing Hurst's shot rebound off the bar, instead of heading for a corner, had chested the ball down and brought it upfield. Would referee Dienst have been so keen to consult linesman Bakhramov with the ball still in play?

Trixie's house in Mayfield Road, Dagenham, not far from the birthplace of Moore and Ramsey, is still there. Uncle Frank died of a heart attack, aged 45, a year later.

This fan joined the *Ilford Recorder* newspaper as a junior reporter the Monday after the final. The *Recorder*'s proximity to

West Ham meant that I was, from time to time, able to meet Moore, Hurst and Peters and even penned Moore's weekly column when the Sports Editor was on holiday. That was privilege enough, but nothing like being able to say I was there the day England won the World Cup.

After 1966, Greaves played for England just three more times before announcing his international career was over and not long before England were heading to Mexico for the defence of the World Cup, came the irony of ironies as Peters moved across London to join Spurs in a deal that saw Greaves come the other way to partner Hurst, the player who had kept him out the final four years earlier. Greaves's debut came away to Manchester City and he scored twice, but it was never the same for him as it was at Tottenham.

His last England appearance had come three years earlier in a 1–0 win against Austria in Vienna and during a brief time at the Hammers, one of the east end's greatest goalscorers played only 38 games, scoring 13 times. His career ended near to where he was born and his life descended into alcoholism, a fight that he won.

Peters progressed to win honours at Tottenham with two League Cup triumphs and he spent five years at White Hart Lane before moving to Norwich in a deal worth £50,000. He ended his playing days with Sheffield United, a club where he became player-manager.

In 1972, Hurst moved to Stoke, spending three years in the Potteries before joining West Bromich Albion. The growing lure of America, and the money it offered, was becoming attractive to many players as the USA tried to make a breakthrough in the game, and Hurst moved across the Atlantic to play for Seattle Sounders and then returned to Britain, moving into management. He was put in charge at Chelsea between 1979 and 1981, but he was replaced by John Neal after failing to win anything at Stamford Bridge.

Today, all three remain high-profile figures, from television work to promotion, to re-telling their story from 1966. For two of them, it was the greatest English football story ever told, for one, the story that he had to live with for the rest of his life.

As the World Cup in Japan drew closer in the summer of 2002, the England team of 1966 were reunited for a number of special promotions and they are still very much involved in football.

It was fitting that in West Ham's first home match after the death of Moore, against Wolves on 6 March 1993, Hurst and Peters led the tributes on the pitch. They carried out a wreath made into the shape of a West Ham shirt with the No. 6 on the back and placed it in the centre circle as Upton Park hushed for a two-minute silence. No one wore the No. 6 shirt for West Ham that day and there was a campaign to retire it forever. That did not happen, but the tribute to Moore came when his old club named their new stand after him. Floral tributes surrounded the main gates as the east end paid its respects, led on that day by the other two players who had been in the England trio from the east end.

As for Ramsey, not everyone inside the FA liked him, but the England manager who won the World Cup does not necessarily need friends in high places. When the side failed to reach the 1974 finals, he was sacked.

But his place and his success could not be removed from the fabric of English football, no matter what the outcome was. The area where he originated was fast developing into a football hotbed and one road in particular was doing its best to bring through a succession of big names, some of whom still dominate the headlines today . . .

## 5. The Bonham Road Boys

THE ROAD WHERE TERENCE FREDERICK VENABLES USED TO LIVE
is almost a mile long, with 18 'sleeping policemen', a sign saying 'No
Games' on a grass verge halfway down it and a banner outside the
junior school that he used to attend that reads: 'Show us you care, park
elsewhere.' Which is all rather ironic because the talent that Venables
showed even as a youngster, which led him to represent his country at
every level, from junior through to his two full international caps, was
honed by playing football in the streets because of the lack of cars.

Venable's talent has made him one of football's great characters,
who became the manager of one of the biggest club sides in Europe,
Barcelona, and, after spending this summer observing the World Cup
in Japan from afar as a television pundit, returned to the game that has
been his life by taking the manager's job at Leeds, one of the top posts
in the country, at the age of 59. So his priorities have gone back to
team selection, another fitting role for Venables – the street where he
lived made sure he was good at it.

While Venables might have become its most famous resident, the
roll call of the boys who have emerged from Bonham Road is like
announcing a team line-up: Ken Brown, Les Allen (father of Clive
and Bradley), Dennis Allen (father of Martin), Dean Coney (the
former England Under-21 striker who played for Fulham and,
Norwich), with a few streets away, Sir Alf Ramsey as their 'manager'.

It is a link that has remained as strong in the modern era as it was
50 years ago because when Venables and Brown, the former Norwich
manager, made a nostalgic trip back to Dagenham for a promotions

event in 1993, a post with England was the outcome for Brown. At the time Venables was favourite to become the national coach and after he was given that job, he offered Brown the chance to be one of the scouts for the team.

Brown spent three weeks at the World Cup in Japan and South Korea, travelling to matches to watch England's next opponents and reporting back to the new manager Sven-Goran Eriksson.

'It all started from seeing Terry in Dagenham. There was a charity event and from there it took me to this year's World Cup,' Brown says. 'Nowadays Terry and I talk a lot about Bonham Road, about his mum and dad. She was a dancing instructor, and she actually taught me to dance. I still can't dance but perhaps there was no hope!'

While Brown was set to pursue a career in the woodwork business, Venables had one desire. 'I can't think of anything I ever wanted to be except a footballer,' recalls Venables. 'It was my only love from as far back as I can remember. I would always be playing with the bigger lads. In fact, I am about the same height now as I was then. I never grew much after that.'

Apart from kicking the ball around in Bonham Road itself, there were two parks nearby to play in, Valence and Parsloes. They have left Venables with memories of how an individual could adapt his game. As boys, he and his peers developed skills that would remain with them forever and the yardsticks that were set then have been maintained.

'What I do remember well is how amazing the standard was and how, whenever you wanted a game, you would always get one,' says Venables. 'There was no limit on the numbers of players either. What always struck me as a youngster when we used to play was how good the players were.

'Often, I could just meet up with a friend and we would go over the park for a game; there would be a guarantee that a match would be taking place and the people who joined late would become known as "pudding and beef".

'We would go towards where the game was on and someone would shout out, "Pudding on that team, beef on the other!" and you would be in. Sometimes the matches would be 20-a-side. We would play football after school all the time, as a matter of course, and the games used to be such a big part of our lives.'

Like Noel Cantwell, Venables is a great believer that playing on different surfaces, such as the road, can teach you good habits. 'It can bring the best out of you,' he said. 'Football is a game where players were made to stay on their feet and if you are playing on hard surfaces, you cannot dive in on the ground because you will end up with cuts and bruises.

'Also, the ball will speed off on a harder area, so you have to have greater control if you are not playing on grass, and with that greater control comes a way of learning a technique that, when transferred to the match scenario on a pitch, can make you stand out. It can teach youngsters good habits.'

Venables was quickly picking up good habits when he arrived, with his football ambitions in tow, as a pupil, at the age of 11, at Lymington High School, one street away from Bonham Road. Today, outside the plot where the school was, two iron gates are locked together and behind them is a mass of overgrown grass that has been left untended since the education institution was shut down.

Venables always did his best to stay in touch with the person who inspired him the most during his days there – his physical education teacher, Mr Jackson. It is the classic story: influences arrive from different quarters, the expected direction from parents, what you learn at school and the people you meet on the way. No one person can have a direct effect on guiding you one way or the other. But Venables will still never forget the teacher that had more influence than any of the others.

'During the Second World War Mr Jackson was a pilot and he lost a leg when the plane he was in suffered a fire in the cockpit and crashed,' recalls Venables. 'I will always remember how supportive he was of me during my time at Lymington. He thought a lot of me and, though he left to go to live in Warwickshire, we used to keep in touch by letter.

'He was so enthusiastic when it came to football. He was strict but he had a fantastic charisma about him and he was someone that it was very easy to look up to.

'He was a very impressive, commanding-looking man and, during games, he would stand on the touchline in a suit and with his walking stick and you knew that he was watching you intently. What develops at school can lead to the completion of what you want in life and if you have an influence like this, along with the collection of the influences you have in your career, it can be a big help.'

From the Lymington school team came selection for the district of Dagenham side in 1957, when he found himself in the same team as Martin Peters, who progressed to join West Ham and score one of those goals in that match at Wembley in July 1966. 'When we played together in that team,' recalls Venables, 'Martin was a left-back.' This is not surprising considering the variety of positions Peters played in at the time.

The scouts were on the scene and Venables had a selection of clubs that he used to train with: Spurs, Chelsea and West Ham. It was a time of development at West Ham, particularly in their youth system, which still exists today. As Bobby Moore once did, Venables arrived for training every Tuesday and Thursday at a time when the man who would captain England to glory in 1966 had just begun finding his way into the first team.

'He was a bit older than me,' recalls Venables. 'We would go to the café near the ground after training and it was in there that I met Bobby for the first time. We had egg on toast and he would not let me pay for it. I have never forgotten that because things like that will stay with you forever.

'But going to clubs like West Ham and Chelsea meant there was a greater chance of progressing into the first team because the Arsenals and Tottenhams of this world would buy big players from elsewhere.'

The choice had to be made. Venables, a midfielder, had made friends through training who chose both Upton Park and Stamford Bridge. In the summer of 1958, he opted for Chelsea and so began a career that has fulfilled the strong ambition which he had since childhood.

Venables is the only player to have progressed to every level with England. He won caps as a schoolboy and youth, the amateur England team and the old Under-23 level before his first-team debut on 21 October 1964, in Brussels at the age of 21, in a 2–2 against Belgium, selected by his one-time near-neighbour in Dagenham, Ramsey.

Venables played for England only once more, two months later in a 1–1 draw with Holland in Amsterdam. The following year he moved to Tottenham.

Three years later he went to QPR and then in 1974 he joined Crystal Palace under Malcolm Allison; two years after that he moved into the side of the game where he has made his name: management. By 1984, after four years at QPR where he progressed from manager to managing director, the lure of Barcelona beckoned for the boy from Bonham Road.

Today, Venables still has his doubters. People say he has not achieved enough to justify being in the frame for so many jobs, even though he won the Spanish League and took Barcelona to the final of the European Cup before being sacked. He returned to Spurs in 1987 as manager and four years later, along with leading businessman Alan Sugar, took over the club.

But in 1993, it all turned sour with Venables, who had been made chief executive, being sacked by Sugar in a dispute that went all the way to the High Court. Yet ultimately it did not affect the way the football world perceived Venables, because a year later he was given the top job in the country. Inside the game, people talk about Venables as being one of the finest motivators in the business because of his presence and ability to bring the best out of players.

When he finally completed the set of England honours, from schoolboy to manager, in 1994, he guided the team through a period of no competitive games in the run-up to Euro '96, where they reached the semi-finals, losing to Germany on penalties at Wembley.

And now he is back, with Leeds, a new venture, a new target

audience to please and a new challenge for Venables who climbed onto every rung of the England ladder from the days when he would play football in the streets.

He has remained one of the highest-profile figures in the English game, even after leaving the national post, with his work as a television pundit with ITV and has never been far from having an involvement in the sport.

Venables is sure that where he came from had something to do with it. 'Some areas are stronger than others and the working-class areas do provide more footballers than others; you don't get too many players from Weybridge for example,' he says. 'At least you did not in the past, because the working-class areas were the breeding grounds. You did not have golf or tennis clubs and generally the majority of parents would say to their children that a career in football is a risky business but now with the way the game has gone, and the money that has come into it, maybe we shall start getting some players from the middle-class parts.

'Yet football has changed. It has become such a huge thing, it has become so professional that now it is that much harder to get to the top. Not only that but because of the way the game has grown into a worldwide sport . . . youngsters wanting to get to the top now have much greater competition from players in Europe and beyond, and you have to be that much better and even more dedicated to reach your goals.

'But I am sure that the area where you grow up does have a big effect upon on you and where your life takes you. For example, if Bobby Charlton had been taken to America when he was a youngster, would he have become a footballer and reached the heights that he did? Maybe, but possibly not. Where you develop can drive you forward.

'I have never lost my enthusiasm for the game – it has always been there – and I don't expect I ever will.'

Bonham Road had set the standards even before Venables was born, with the Allen brothers, Dennis and Les. Both were born in Dagenham and after Les had joined Tottenham from Chelsea in 1959, he scored 27 goals as Spurs won the Double. That was in the 1960–61 season and 36 years later, Les's son Clive became a hero at White Hart Lane when he scored 49 goals and ended up being managed by Venables, who had been his boss as QPR.

And people say football is not one big family.

Les's brother Dennis did not reach the same heights, spending the majority of his career at Reading.

Bonham Road itself is broken into three parts and for Ken Brown, who became the West Ham centre-half alongside Moore, it contains a lifetime of memories. Though he was nine years older than Venables, they lived only eight doors apart and when they returned to the area in the early 1990s, not only did their visit rekindle memories about the place but it led Brown to a new footballing task as England scout.

He spends most days now helping at a leisure centre near his home in Norwich that he owns shares in, but, this summer, he was selected to go to the World Cup. Brown, now 68, is now one of five scouts that have been weaned into the current England set-up from the days when Venables was in charge, the others being Ted Buxton, Cantwell, John Sillett and Frank Clark.

When Eriksson took charge, he could not believe that five men with such vast football experience between them were in these positions, revealing he knew no other country that had established such a strong scouting base.

Brown recalls: 'Terry and I were in Dagenham just before he got the England job. He told me there was a strong possibility that he might be made manager and asked me if I would like to "come and do a bit for him". He said there would be no money involved and I told him: "That's bloody good!" But all expenses would be paid and he would need someone to look at players.

'It was great to be given a role and then when Sven came in, Dave Sexton [England senior team scouting co-ordinator] and I were at

West Ham and he asked me if I would still be doing it. I said "Sure" and he told me he had spoken to Sven, who was amazed that we have people willing to do this.

'Sven is a great fellow, and his strength is that he does not complicate things. He plays people in the same position for the country as they do for their club, he keeps it simple and if you are good enough, you are in.

'This year we were even watching pre-season games, and it is not always about watching teams. We sometimes go to see particular players, we give marks out of four and they have even started to pay us for the time that we are away. It has been fabulous to be involved. It has kept me going because I am not sure what involvement I would have had in football.'

If Brown had ceased to be involved in football, it would have been a loss to the game he has served so well. He spent much of his time in Japan travelling around with David Platt, the England Under-21 manager, watching the country's opponents for the forthcoming games.

'The way the scouting takes place has grown. I did the same job for Glenn Hoddle and then Kevin Keegan after Terry had left and now Sven has come in; the FA are building a database so whoever is manager can just go to the files to see any particular player of any team.'

While Brown deals directly with Sexton, the former Manchester United and England Under-21 manager, he has at least had a little bit more contact with the manager than he did in the 1950s with the man who was going to lead the country to their greatest football moment.

'I used to travel to training at West Ham on a bus with the legendary Dick Walker, who was the Hammers centre-half at the time,' recalls Brown. 'I did not know Alf Ramsey, even though he used to live near us in Bonham Road.

'We got on this bus one morning, sat down and Dick turned around and said: "Hello, Alf." He replied: "Hello, Richard, how are you?" Dick then said: "This is Ken Brown: he will play for England one day."

'So the two of them were talking away and as we got off at Barking Station, Alf said it was nice to meet me. Once the bus pulled away, Dick turned to me and said: "Get a pint of brown ale inside him and he will start to talk like you and me!"'

Walker was right. Brown did play for England – once, in 1960 against Northern Ireland when he was selected by Walter Winterbottom. He was never chosen again, but his brief experience again shows how football has changed, even in the length of time the England team spent together before a tournament compared to now, let alone the manner in which the players would congregate.

Brown laughs when he thinks back to how it worked. 'England had about three internationals each year and it is so strange when you look at the scenario before games then and now and when you think of the boys who went to Dubai to prepare before this year's World Cup.

'When I was selected, I was notified that I had to meet the officials at a hotel in Mill Hill. There I was, sitting down on one side of the room, someone else was in the other part, and we did not know each other. There were about five new caps including Ron Springett and we met up on the Monday and the game was on the Wednesday.

'I would suspect that the majority of new arrivals that come into the England squad now would know the rest of the lads. But not then. We did not play as many games and the profile was not as high as it is nowadays.

'The game went okay but we did not have another international until the following season. By then West Ham's form had started to dip and I was left out. But I played once – at least I could say that.'

Dick Walker was an integral part of the West Ham side in the mid-1950s and used to walk down Bonham Road every morning to visit his sister before catching the bus to Upton Park. 'Everyone would say, "There is Dick Walker" as he went by, but no one would ever go up to speak to him,' says Brown, who used to play for a street team called Neville United, made up from the boys in the area. Football was a leisure activity to him because he was working in a woodwork factory. They would play matches against West Ham's youth team and regularly beat them, leading to their scout trying to persuade Brown to go and play for them.

'I said to him "Why would I want to play for West Ham? We keep beating you!"' recalls Brown. 'We had a well-run team [managed] by a guy from a little council house and I had practically qualified to be a wood machinist. In the meantime, West Ham kept asking me to play in the London Midweek League; in the end I did and they paid my expenses.

'Eventually the company I was working for in Stratford started to get a bit funny about me playing football every week, so I told them what they could do with their job.'

Brown started training at West Ham every Tuesday and Thursday in 1951 and by walking out on his job in the factory, he walked straight into a new career as a professional footballer . . . to his total surprise.

'I went in on this particular Tuesday and I told them that I had not got a job,' he recalls. 'Ted Fenton was the manager and the people who owned West Ham at the time were in the woodwork business and I thought they might give me something.

'Ted said I should stay in the dressing-room after training and wait for him and I thought he had forgotten all about me because I was sitting there for ages.'

Eventually Fenton came back – and Brown was left stunned.

'It's all okay, son,' said Fenton.

'Great, you have got me a job,' replied Brown, thinking he was back in work, now for the owners of West Ham.

'We are going to sign you on professional forms,' said Fenton.

'But I am not quite sure what that means; does it mean that all I do is play football?'

'Yes.'

'What, all the time?'

'Yes.'

Brown says now: 'I could not believe it, there was no talk about money and I ran virtually all the way back to Dagenham to tell my parents. Dad said, "That's brilliant," and Mum said, "Ooh, that is nice."'

It was then that Dick Walker, the man no one dared talked to, became a close friend of Brown, his bus and tea companion from Bonham Road every morning. Fenton gave Walker instructions to chaperon Brown because they both played in the same position and the manager believed he had the ability to progress.

'Dick asked me if I knew where his sister lived in Bonham Road because we would go to work together,' recalls Brown. 'I told him I did and he said that he leaves exactly at nine in the morning so I should be there waiting for him after he has popped in to see her from his home in Romford.

'On the first day, there I am at 8.55, to be sure I am not late. I dare not knock and right on nine, Dick comes out, marching off down the road with me almost running to try to catch him up. He told me he wanted me there at nine, not before, but the next day I was a minute late and he had already gone. When I caught up with him, he said, "Are you never going to get it right?" The education I received from him was unbelievable. Everyone knew Dick Walker.'

Walker agreed they would have a deal: one day Brown would pay for their bus fare and tea once they arrived at the ground and the next day, Walker would pay – and he had it all planned out.

As Brown tells the story, he just about manages to keep a straight face.

'On the first day, the bus comes along and I pay for two to Upton Park and then I buy the teas once we have reached the café,' he says. 'The next day, it is Dick's turn to pay. We get to the bus stop but he says he does not want the first bus that comes along. It goes past us and I think, "What is he up to?"

'The next one arrives, on we get and there is a woman bus conductor. She says, "Hello Dick," and we are sitting down and he has not paid the fares. All the way down she is talking to him and he is giving her the chat. I said to him that he did not pay the fare and he replied that as she knew him, it would be okay.

'Then we go to the café by the ground and he shouts "Phil, two teas here, please." He did not pay for those either; that is how much he was respected.

'Anyway, next day, he told me to get the fares. I said "Wait a minute, you didn't get them yesterday." He said, "What do you mean?" I said, "Did we not have a deal, one day you, one day me?" And he replied that we did, and yesterday was his turn. The fact he did not have to pay did not come into it. What a character.'

Walker did all he could to guide Brown, as he was asked to by Fenton.

'Dick was always on about presentation,' says Brown. 'He told me that as I was in the first team, I must not let anyone down. We had a gym at the club and I was doing some fitness work in there when Dick came through and asked me what I was doing and why I was wearing my match shorts. He told me to get them off, informing me that they had been pressed and I was creasing them for the game. He said: "If you can't play, at least look the part."'

The only time Brown was sent off in his career came during his spell doing national service in Aldershot when he was 18. He had been seconded there while at West Ham. 'It was the one time I could not leave at the weekend, I was playing in a game at the base and this fellow came up behind me and gave me an almighty kick,' he recalls. 'I shouted out "Jesus Christ" and the referee sent me off. I said "But, but . . ." and he said, "No buts." And why was I sent off? Because the referee was a vicar!'

West Ham did their best to help Brown stay at the top of his game during his time away. He had to serve two years' national service, and this is an another example of the change in priorities between then and now: can you imagine a modern footballer being available only on Saturdays?

Brown was in the medical corps in Aldershot and his sergeant major ensured he was fit. 'At one time I was his runner and he used to make me lie down in his office, on my back and do exercises. He would ensure I was keeping fit for West Ham duty without me even knowing it. Ted Fenton had spoken to him and between them, they were making sure I was staying trim.'

In one of Brown's first matches in the first team, away to Rotherham, the match was being drawn when West Ham conceded a penalty with five minutes to go. Goalkeeper Ernie Gregory saved it brilliantly, tipping the ball around the post. 'I ran up to him and said, "Ernie, that was magnificent." But he told me to go away saying: "Son, I should have caught it,"' recalls Brown.

Brown was at West Ham for 17 years, leaving in 1968, having won the FA Cup and European Cup-Winners' Cup in matches played at Wembley. He partnered Bobby Moore before progressing to a successful career as a manager that included leading Norwich to the 1985 League Cup with a 1–0 victory over Sunderland at Wembley.

And all from being a child who used to play sport in Bonham Road, just like his near neighbour Terry Venables and many more before and after him.

'There were no cars and when we used to play cricket, there was a drain hole where we would put the stumps; even when winter came, we used to play cricket,' Brown says. 'There were no worries about going outside and cars were never really heard of. Now you cannot walk in the road anymore, let alone play in it.'

If you do, you will find a sign that says 'No games', despite it being a road that produced one of the game's highest-profile servants in Terence Frederick Venables.

But he was not the only manager that the end can be proud of . . .

# 6. The Thing about Harry

HARRY REDKNAPP WAS BORN ON 2 MARCH 1947 IN POPLAR, A suburb of east London that, during his childhood, was among the poorest of all the parts of this corner of England. The effects of the Blitz during the Second World War might have drawn people together, but that did not necessarily mean that their lives were any better. Rebuilding was slow, regeneration had no time limit and the effects of the War and what the east end of London had gone through were still so vivid in the minds of eastenders, who, as much as they tried, had no way of blanking out what had happened to them.

Poplar and the immediate surrounding areas, such as West Ham and Mile End, came under attack from the first German assault on 7 September 1940, a night that changed everything for the people of Britain. On that evening, more than 400 people died, over 1,500 were injured and the amount left homeless was countless. The Blitz would last for more than eight months, raid after terrifying raid leaving fire burning through the streets. Assertions have been made that the blazes that raged were greater than those of the Great Fire itself in the heart of the capital almost 300 years before. Even to this day it has not been erased from the collective memory, because a strip of land, Mile End Park, has been built on foundations that were damaged heavily during the constant barrage of air raids and is the site where the first VII rocket that was launched by the Germans landed on 14 February 1944.

Now there are plans to build a memorial in Whitechapel to Queen Elizabeth, the late Queen Mother, who famously visited the area and stood side by side with the people of London after an air raid rocked the city.

What emerged at the end of the War and in the years that followed was a need for some restoration among those who had taken as much suffering as they could face. Security in a job was essential, and a home was top priority as slowly the east end regained its footing. So not long after Harry Redknapp entered the world on that Sunday in March less than two years after the war had ended, his future life was decided: he was down to become a docker. 'That is the way it worked then,' he says. 'My father [whose name is also Harry] had been a prisoner of war. When life got back to some normality, he went into the docks and the succession to the son was just acceptable.'

They ended up living in a flat in one of the many tower blocks that emerged during the rebuilding of the area post-1945. Theirs was on the Burdett Estate, a typical high rise in the heart of Stepney. The area had taken its toll of unimaginable suffering. There were not many cars around, and so much of life was centred on the home. Yet this foundation provided the essential character-building quality that has turned the boy who was destined to work in the docks into one of the highest-profile, most popular, and, significantly, down-to-earth characters in English football today.

Harry Redknapp is the manager of Portsmouth, a team in the First Division with the ambition to make it into the Premiership. He lives on the south coast, but his heart is still in one place. England's eastenders can have no greater member of its community than "Arry' himself, a cockney who speaks his mind, and if people do not like it, then they are going to have to get used to it.

As a boy Harry supported Arsenal and then progressed to play for West Ham, the club where he was always destined to go, once football became the road his life was set to follow. He was there for 11 years as a player, a tenacious outside-right who wore the claret-and-blue shirt 146 times and became one of the club's most popular representatives because of an ethic he has carried with him from the days when he first kicked a ball right up to this very moment: 'It is only a game.'

'However much money floats around football today, and we don't need to even ponder that it is anything less than extortionate, I have never forgotten the fundamental, basic, bottom line,' he says. 'But it is a game that draws a passion out of me that sometimes I cannot explain. I have always had a genuine love of football; I would go anywhere to watch it. Even now, it is a living that is not hard work to me, it is something I always enjoy doing. But the east end makes me the way I am towards my life in football. I am streetwise because I am from an area where you had to be streetwise to survive.'

Life was just so different then. Football was not just an escape, it was almost the only thing to do for a child like Redknapp when he arrived home from school. As he says: 'Television was limited. You had two stations, maybe just one. Our first television was a nine-inch screen, but we hooked a magnifying glass over the front of it to make it 12-inch. That was wonderful, it was a different world to what we have now, so the alternative was to go and play football.

'When I was a kid, you had the bath in front of the fire and you had an outside toilet. It never surprises me how many footballers and boxers come from the east end of London because you are brought up tough, you are made to handle yourself and you are made to learn about life very quickly because the area made you do it. There was no messing; people had been through enough and it was time to be wise to what was going on. The area wanted to move on and though we did not have much, we had to protect what we did have.

'But it was fantastic if you were a kid where we lived. There were so many other youngsters around that you were never short of a game of football. Wherever you looked, someone had a ball, there was always a game going on; on the grass behind the flats, on the school playground and in the area exactly where we lived.'

Everyone's life has influences that at the time might not seem to be affecting you, but in later years prove the significant moments that have changed your approach and the direction in which you might be heading. Redknapp gives a number of reasons for what he achieved. One of those life-changing moments came when he was eight, and perhaps turned him away from the dockyards to the football pitch – and all because of a mis-kick.

Of the boys on the Burdett, one of Harry's closest friends was Colin Mackleworth, a goalkeeper who, like Redknapp, ultimately ended up playing for West Ham but never cemented such a reputation. Back in 1955, the routine was simple: home from school, out with the ball and the match would begin. They would play as much as they could and in a flat overlooking where they were kicking the ball around on the estate, a man called Albert Chamberlain, a docker, would watch.

It was in April of that year, and in the middle of one of these games, that Redknapp mis-hit a shot. 'The ball went near Albert's window,' he recalls. 'Within a second out he came and we thought: "That's it, end of our football games." We were only eight at the time and we were so worried about what he was going to do with us, we were ready to run because we all thought that he had come to chase us off. Incredibly, we could not have been more wrong. There was a whole group of us, the regular boys who would play each night, and as we waited to be told off by Albert, he left us all with our mouths wide open. "I have been watching you play," he said. "I am going to start a team up, and would you all like to be in it?"'

He made arrangements for them to join one of the main leagues around at the time, the Regents Boys, but there was no division for them to enter at their age group, so they went into the Under-11s. Each Sunday it made quite a picture, the Pied Piper Albert and his flock marching halfway across London for a game of football. Matches were normally played on the pitches at Regents Park, which meant a two-hour journey on two trains and a bus. Albert, with a bag of balls over his shoulder, was followed by the squad of 16, who knew that, if they were lucky, they would return home happy to have lost just 10–0.

Being two years out of their age group meant a weekly drubbing, but Redknapp will never forget the half-time team talks that Albert would give the boys, normally when they were trailing 5–0. 'Albert always had faith. He would say "Don't worry, we'll be OK." I was always cheeky,' says Redknapp. 'I would answer him back by replying: "Albert, what a load of cobblers, how are we going to win?" He would reply: "We will sort it" . . . and we'd lose 10–0.'

They were the only official team from their estate and in an attempt to plug the leaking of so many goals, they brought in some ringers, older boys who made a startling difference. In a matter of time, the Burdett Boys had won the league, then the cup, and progressed on a run of five years without losing a game.

Sometimes they would play matches at the 'Mecca' of Hackney Marshes, and whatever the age of a side, a team that wins matches for fun, as Burdett started to do, will always come to the fore. The Marshes was the ultimate joint to pick up a footballer; scouts would go over there on a Sunday morning and be spoilt for choice, always collecting the names of one or two boys who had the potential to make it.

As the Burdett Boys were maturing, their talent was becoming noticed: Mackleworth, Redknapp, George Jacks, Roger Hoy and a striker called Terry Reardon were selected to play for East London Boys, an area side comprising the top local talent. That stepped up the standards, and in turn increased the attraction, the opposition and ultimately the quality of competitions they were playing in.

By now, Redknapp was 11 and a regular member of the East London Under-12 team that in 1958 progressed to a cup final played at Millwall's Den ground in south London against Wandsworth Boys. He had a good game, showing some fine control and giving it his all. East London won and afterwards, he thought nothing more of his own performance until an imposing, good-looking man came up to him to ask if his dad was around. He thought it was one of his father's friends. Harry Senior was called over, the two men began talking and the young Harry realised the man was Dick Walker, the former West Ham centre-half, and at the time a scout for Tottenham.

He had been watching Redknapp and was so impressed with what he saw that he wanted to arrange for him to go to White Hart Lane to meet the manager, Bill Nicholson, and arrange for a trial.

Nicholson was one of the biggest names in management in Britain. He was a blunt Yorkshireman who believed in traditional values and got the best out of what became one the greatest Tottenham team of them all; led by Danny Blanchflower, they became one of the first sides of the modern era to achieve the Double of winning both the League and the FA Cup in the same season in 1960–61. And now the Redknapps were going to meet Nicholson.

The two Harrys set off on the journey, a train from Mile End to Liverpool Street and then on to Spurs, where they were welcomed into the stadium and Bill Nicholson appeared. A friendly greeting and the conversation began.

'Where do you play, son,' said Nicholson.

'Outside-right, Mr Nicholson,' came the reply.

'Do you score goals?'

'Not many, Mr Nicholson.'

'Son, I only know one outside-right who does not score goals and his name is Stanley Matthews. Are you going to be as good as him?'

'I doubt it.'

'Well, you better start scoring some goals then!'

Redknapp was welcomed to Spurs for regular training after school each week and he was not alone, because Reardon had already been earmarked by them and was there too.

Reardon was considered the best schoolboy in the country but in the end he moved out of football and became a taxi driver at the age of 23. He was wanted by so many clubs, Redknapp recalls, that he played, at the age of 12, for the East London Boys' Under-15 team in the English Schools final at Old Trafford and the place was packed with scouts watching him. For the young Mr Redknapp, a career in football was looking increasing likely too because every one of the big teams in London had some link with him.

Spurs might have had him training with them, but there were no ties. Redknapp was in no rush. But 1958 was significant for him in another way. His dad was an Arsenal fan and along with his Uncle Jim, Redknapp would go to Highbury to see the home games.

On 1 February 1958, Manchester United were the visitors – the Busby Babes team of Duncan Edwards, Dennis Viollet, Bobby Charlton and the players who were icons of that generation.

It was an astonishing game, United winning 5–4 before a disbelieving crowd. Edwards gave Manchester United the lead and by half-time the visitors were 3–0 ahead. But an incredible turnaround at the start of the second half saw Arsenal draw level before Tommy Taylor and Dennis Violet put United clear again before the home side responded once more.

Five days later, on their way back from a European Cup quarter-final match against Red Star Belgrade, their plane refuelled in Munich and on take off it crashed, killing eight of the players, including Taylor and Edwards.

'It still sends a chill through me when I think of what happened to them. I don't know if it is for that reason but the game at Arsenal was the best match I have ever seen,' says Redknapp. 'I would not like to guess at the amount of games I have been involved in but nothing can match that one in 1958. It was the most amazing 90 minutes of football imaginable. I did not need my appetite whetted any further for the game but if I ever did, that match would have done it for me.'

Football was fast becoming the direction Harry's career was taking him, which was good because otherwise he would not have made it through his education at Sir Humphrey Gilbert School in Stepney.

'You did not have too many choices in those days,' he says. 'There were grammar schools or, if you were a real idiot, you would go to a secondary modern, so you can guess where I ended up. The place was a madhouse, absolutely full of nutters. I had no education because I was one of those cheeky kids that the area seemed to produce and all I did at school was play football and mess around. I could never explain to anyone what type of schooling I had. It was not real.'

The playground was on the roof, so to find a pitch for organised football as part of physical education, they would travel to playing fields in an area called Goresbrook in Dagenham. The Green Line bus service operated the route and the traffic was so bad that by the time they reached Goresbrook, they would have to head straight back to be in time for the end of the school day. They would have about ten minutes of actually playing, so if Redknapp's game was ever going to be improved by soccer at school, there was not a chance of it happening that way.

The extent of how rough the school was, and to what extent toughness was valued in the area, was demonstrated one day when Sir Humphrey Gilbert had been drawn to play an extraordinarily named school from Leyton, Hay Curry, in an Under-15s match where the referee was Redknapp's metalwork teacher, Mr Harris. The man in black ended the day black and blue because players from Hay Curry beat him up when he left after the match. He was shoved off his bike, which they then kicked. 'It was unbelievable.'

With no grass pitch, Sir Humphrey's 'home' was a red gravel area. Beforehand, Mr Harris would bring out a big stick and mark in the surface how the tactics would work. He would write a big 'w' and a big 'm' and that was their formation. 'Then he would tell one of us to do this, another to do that and not one of us knew what the hell he was talking about,' says Redknapp.

'It was a breeding ground, it hardened you, it allowed you to take knocks, climb above it and think that if the chance arises I am going to prove I can do something with my life. Maybe it is the reason why I progressed in football, why I chose to forget the madhouse and set my vision on making it as a player.'

The scouts watched him and the rest of the Burdett and East London boys regularly, but no schoolboy terms had yet been signed with Spurs. At 14, Harry was looking at leaving Sir Humphrey Gilbert the following year. It was summer holiday time and business as usual, with the boys playing as much football as they could on the estate.

One night, the doorbell rang at the Redknapp home and standing outside was Tommy Docherty, the manager of Chelsea, whom the Reknapps had watched regularly when he played for Arsenal.

'I was gobsmacked,' recalls Harry. 'I was only 14 at the time and Dad and I were football nutters. Now, standing at our door, was Tommy Docherty.'

During his time at West Ham in particular, Redknapp became legendary for the amount of transfer dealings he became involved in. Does any player inside the top two divisions operate without an agent? How rare is a deal thrashed out between manager and manager, without any interfering parties or the story emerging in the press in some form? It is almost non-existent. The memory brings a wild chuckle from Redknapp because when he thinks back to what Docherty did then, it was beyond belief. He had come around to their house to personally persuade Harry to sign for Chelsea. His potential had moved from the Marshes to west London and Docherty knew that he had to be quick because so many of the capital's clubs were after him.

Well, after years of shouting from the stands at Highbury and not getting a response, the Redknapps' moment had arrived.

'Tommy had come to sign me, and Dad and I ended up battering him all night about Arsenal and why he did this as a player and why didn't he do that during his time there. Can you believe it?' he says. 'We spent the night making up for all those times Tommy could not have heard us during games.'

But as hard as Docherty tried, nothing was going to be definite with Redknapp, who was training with Spurs and seemed likely to be happy to join them. But the very next night, the doorbell went again and this time on the doorstep was Phil Woosnam, the captain of West Ham. 'It was ridiculous,' says Redknapp. 'Even the players were now coming around, to try to sell me the reasons why I should join their club. I don't know why they were all chasing after me.'

What eventually swayed him was not the kudos of having a particular manager or player in their home but the fact that Redknapp's friend Colin Mackleworth had already joined on schoolboy terms for West Ham, the local club, the team where the eastenders went and where, when Redknapp had been for trials, a certain manager had made an immediate impression.

'Colin was there and they had a very good reputation for giving kids a chance,' he says. 'As a manager, Ron Greenwood was magnificent. He would always come upstairs and talk to the parents after the football was finished; he made it seem like a family club, so I knew it was the place for me.'

Arsenal ended up not being in the picture. Even though he was a fan, his dad would tell him: 'They are one of the posher clubs and you can't play for them unless you use your knife and fork properly!'

Much of Redknapp's inspiration came from his father, who watches as much football as he can. 'From where he lives in London, he can see pitches, and if the floodlights are on, he is over there watching a game; he is 77 and still football barmy.'

The deal was done and Harry Redknapp signed professionally for West Ham on 15 March 1964, making his debut in the first team on 23 August 1965 in a 1–1 draw at home to Sunderland and creating a wonderful name for himself. He left in 1975 for a brief spell at Brentford and then went to Bournemouth, where he returned in 1982 as manager, the first step on the ladder that took him back to Upton Park in 1992 as assistant to Billy Bonds. Twelve months later he was given the manager's job himself, before his shock parting of the ways with them in the spring of 2000 at the end of a season where they had just escaped relegation. It was fitting that Redknapp spent so much time in charge of the Hammers, because it allowed him to carry on the tradition that had been set down by Greenwood.

Greenwood, who later progressed to become England manager, leading the country to the 1982 World Cup finals in Spain, had a presence that to this day inspires Redknapp in a way that he will never forget.

'Ron would be at the South-East Counties League on Saturday morning; he would then would go to see the youths and on to the first team in the afternoon,' says Redknapp. 'He wanted to be involved in every part of the club because he knew how important him being there could be, whatever the age group and however tricky it might be for him to make it to all the games.'

In his first season as a schoolboy at the club, West Ham reached the FA Youth Cup final against Liverpool. They lost the first leg 3–1 away from home and by half-time in the second they were trailing 2–1, in front of 25,000 supporters at Upton Park. Tommy Smith, who became a legendary defender, was a member of the Liverpool side who were in such a commanding position in the game. A thrilling turnaround saw the Hammers score four times after the break to win 6–5 on aggregate, lift the cup and allow Redknapp to recall that: 'Ron Greenwood said it was the best night of his life. He had even gone to the semi-final at Wolves when the first team were playing elsewhere on the same day! He just loved watching the youngsters and we ensured he was not disappointed with this win. So when I was at West Ham, I tried to do the same but many managers now do not watch youngsters play at all. I knew how important it was to us to have the first-team manager at the game.

'I have always followed that approach. People will naturally raise their game if the first-team manager is watching and he will also provide them with a special buzz to know they are an important part of the club.

'It is how I work because I remember what it was like when Ron was there; you knew he had come out of his way to see you, so you were not going to let him down . . . even if he was not there, he would definitely want to know what the score was, who scored and who played well.'

There was no dressing-room more proud in the close season of 1966 than that at Upton Park when Bobby Moore, Geoff Hurst and Martin Peters returned after leading England to victory in the World Cup.

Everybody wanted a piece of West Ham after that. They were the biggest draw in the country and the following year, they went on tour to the United States of America for five weeks and then on to Bermuda. But Redknapp will never forget the fashion, started by

Moore, of taking the first team along to youth matches. This became a huge inspiration to the young Redknapp.

'He [Moore] made an immediate impression on us all,' he says. 'Bobby was a different class, as a player and a fellow, and he took to me early on because I was a bit of a jack-the-lad. Even at 16 or 17 I became mates with him and he enjoyed my company as much as I enjoyed his. And from a non-football point of view, he was always like the leader; whatever Bobby did, the others followed.

'It was amazing. If Bobby wore a keyring on the outside of his trousers, then suddenly everyone in the team wore one. That was Bobby and, of course, he did not mind one bit. Everyone looked up to him, I have never met one fellow everyone loved being with as much as they did with Bobby. He had time for everybody, even the kid's team. You just don't get that anymore with all the foreign players that are around in the game now. It is not a criticism, just an example of how things have changed. Bobby had an effect on you, hard to explain really, but it was because of his character that you could not dislike him.

'Even after what Bobby, Geoff and Martin had done in the World Cup, in all that time, they never changed in their attitudes. They had been brought up through the football system, they had been kids cleaning boots, because that was how it was in those days, and now they were three of the biggest names in the game and still the same type of people. It was like that at West Ham, a club full of players from the south and we never knew what a foreigner was, let alone a northerner. When Scotland's Bobby Ferguson joined us, he was probably the first from outside of the area to be in the team.'

It was during the tour to Bermuda that the Hammers, such an attraction, caught the eye of a player called Clyde Best, whose dream was to become a professional footballer. Contact was made with Greenwood from his home in the Bermudan capital of Hamilton, asking for the chance to have a trial with West Ham. The players knew nothing about it, and it had slipped Greenwood's mind until one day in 1968, he was walking off their pitch after training.

'I remember it as vividly as anything,' says Redknapp. 'As we wandered past one of the pitches, there was this guy shooting at goal with the kids in a routine whereby they were taking turns to cross and volley. Suddenly a ball came across, one kid missed it but then the next one comes in to this big fellow who catches it on his chest, turns and smashes it into the top corner.

'I remember Ron turning to me and saying "Did you see that? Who is he?"

'He had a beard and we thought that maybe he was a coach that we did not know. He looked too old to be a player.

'Then, he does it again. Taking the ball down onto his thigh this time and cracking a shot past the goalkeeper.'

Greenwood had forgotten all about Best until he had turned up at the ground.

He was only 18 but as it emerged, he was too good to be in the youth team. Within two months he was on the full side's summer tour and for us, he is the next stop-off point. If there is no greater eastender than Harry Redknapp, there is no greater 'international' eastender than Clyde Best . . .

# 7. Best of Times

THE YOUNG MEN HE WORKS WITH DO NOT KNOW WHO HE IS, AND
that is the way Clyde Best wants it. Fame to him is something that
came because of his talent; now he is just doing a job, one that makes
his success as a footballer seem irrelevant to him. 'There is a passage
in the Bible that tells us "No man is a hero in his own country",' says
Best. 'I am happy with that. I don't want to be a hero, I am here to help
because there is more to life than football.'

The son of a prison warden, Best made more impact on the English
game than any black player before him. He is 51 now and each day he
leaves his home in Somerset on the western tip of the island of
Bermuda to travel to, ironically, a prison's half-way house where he
now works as a counsellor. It is his job to talk to the men about what
he knows best: dealing with life. He prepares inmates who are coming
to the end of their sentences for coping with the outside world again.

'Having played sport, I can relate with a lot of them through it,' he
adds. 'It's like being on the football field on a Saturday afternoon in
the way you deal with people and how you get their respect. If I would
shout at a teammate, he might not respond, and it is the same here. It
is an eye-opening experience and a wonderful challenge for me.'

Few black players received such abuse from opposing fans as Best
after he signed for West Ham, but as we shall discover, he took it and
turned it around to his favour. On his brief visits back to England, he
is often told by some of the black stars of today, such as Ian Wright,
that if it had not been for him, others would not have made it. His
attempts to help others have carried him through most of his life.

'These people might be incarcerated but they are still human beings. You have to respect them and they respect you. Some want to better their lives and move on and it is up to you to help them get through that process unscathed.

'I know what adversity can do to someone, I know how difficult it can be when you're out there somewhere and the abuse is flying but while I do not condone anything these prisoners have done, I am here to help them not to do it again. We try to teach them the basic skills: how to behave, how to get jobs, how to budget the money they earn, how to cook, how to live life. And the satisfaction can be immense. If I can turn around someone's life and stop them from breaking into a person's house, then I have done my part, that is my reward. But as much as helping them, you are saving people's lives at the same time by ensuring they get back their life.'

Often, Clyde Best returns to England and to the corner of the east end where he made his name as a player with West Ham, a martyr to the cause of the first, and probably most intense, racism from fans that the game in this country had seen.

Best likes to call himself an 'eastender' because he was made so welcome by the club and local people during his seven-year stay when, as a midfielder-cum-striker, he played for West Ham 188 times. But he went beyond just pulling on a claret-and-blue shirt each week: it was the dirt that he had to rub off of it at the end that revealed the extent of his task.

Ironically, when England progressed to the quarter-finals of the World Cup in Japan, there were six black players in the starting line-up against Brazil and while Best has no desire to take credit, he knows that what he did made a difference. Even now, racism goes on in the game and he is amazed at the way guilty players escape with such light sentences. 'We are in the twenty-first century now and it seems unbelievable that it can still happen. When the abuse was at its height with me, I had a theory that I carry to this day: the ball does not know the colour of the person who is kicking it. I hope we can solve it, perhaps one day we can just get on with the game. I had no problems carrying the burden and every time I watch games on the television, I see four to five black players at clubs, so I must have left some impact because someone must have seen something in us to allow us to express ourselves.

'I am glad I was able to make a difference. Ian Wright and Cyrille Regis have told me how grateful they are to me because I opened the way. I look upon it as doing a job. I knew I was not doing it just for myself. It was for the people in the factories, on the streets, working in train stations, for people all over the world. If I could make a small difference to the way people looked at us, then it was worth it.'

The rise of racism in football was never greater than in the late 1960s and early 1970s and the fact that Best bore the brunt of it because of his higher than normal profile, a result of his background, makes it all the more surprising that he did not take the first flight back home to Bermuda.

He made his debut in a home game against Arsenal in March 1969. Even when the abuse began to reach its height, his attitude never changed. 'The more they chanted, the more I wanted to get the ball and stick it in the back of the net – what greater answer could there be?' he says. But the racial hatred increased to a level where the police had to be called in before a game because Best received a letter through the post that informed him he would have acid sprayed in his face when he ran through the tunnel. And that was in a home match.

'All these problems, I never let them interfere with me but on this occasion, I was frightened. Names and all the rest was something I could take because I expected it but now this took it on a bit further. In the end nothing happened but before the game, you can imagine how I felt: it was harrowing and I was surrounded by police in the tunnel before we went out. I was like a lap-dog, desperate to break free and get onto the pitch. They never found out who the threat was from, whether or not it was from a home fan or not, but, to this day, I still receive fan mail from people thanking me for making a difference.

'I did not go there on some mission: I went there to play football, the game I knew and loved, but it provides me with a tremendous feeling to realise that maybe something else might have come out of it.'

But what Best cannot comprehend is why the international federation have not hammered out the racism that still goes on in the game now, more than 30 years since one of the first black players to be in a white team emerged onto the scene. It is a problem that has still not been eradicated.

Sol Campbell, the England and Arsenal defender, discovered on a school pitch in Stratford, east London suffered some of the worst abuse from the crowd he had ever heard on the night the team won qualification for the 1998 finals.

They had drawn 0–0 with Italy in Rome and I met Sol a few days later for an exclusive interview for the *Daily Express*. He was still shell-shocked then.

'We were just walking onto the pitch when we heard it,' Campbell said at the time. 'The fans were doing everything they could to put us off, no matter how bad it may have made us feel. It was not the first time I had experienced racial abuse but it is not something you expect any more. You can react either way and I could not keep on thinking about it because I had a job to do . . . I told myself, I have to block these things out.'

Best cringes when he hears such stories and says he would be glad to help FIFA or UEFA, the two international bodies of the sport, find ways of driving racism from the game completely.

He was left incensed when, in the same Olympic Stadium in Rome where Campbell had been abused, Lazio's Sinisa Mihajlovic was banned for only two matches after calling Arsenal's Patrick Vieira 'a black monkey' among other insults during a Champions League match in 2000.

'If UEFA would like me to give them a hand then I would be happy to,' he says. 'The penalties should be so much more severe because if they are not, then it will always be there. What is two games to a player?

'It is something that must be looked at closely because it still goes on and because we are talking about 2002 now. If he was calling him names on the field, he should have been suspended for a year.

'When I joined West Ham, it should never have happened but now . . . I don't tolerate that. We all have red blood and we were all put here together. All we can do now is try to achieve something that I set out to achieve all those years ago. Make a statement. It is surely time that FIFA did something. I will not tolerate it – never. I am here to help because I know more than most what it means to a player.'

The Commission for Racial Equality and the Professional Footballers' Association (PFA) started their 'Kick Racism out of Football' campaign in 1993, and Best claims that he did not receive abuse from fellow professionals because they knew the talent he had and respected him for it.

If Ron Greenwood failed to realise who it was firing those volleys into the top corner on that training day, it did not take him long to discover what he had. 'I must have saved Ron a heck of a load of money,' Best says now.

Greenwood was so eager to give him a trial that West Ham paid for his ticket to come to the club from Bermuda in 1968. He arrived in Britain on a Sunday, expecting to be met at Heathrow Airport, which he wasn't and he took the London Underground to West Ham station and made his own way to Ronald Road, where he stayed with two of West Ham's other black players, Clive and the late John Charles.

'I was 17 and it was quite a step,' he says. 'I always knew what I wanted to do and the European continent was not open to footballers from abroad as it is now.'

Best had shown magnificent talent as a youngster playing in Bermuda, where he had won his first international cap at the age of 15. But the worldwide transfer market was not as it is now; there were few agents, so there was no real way for him to become noticed in Britain.

The young Best's hopes for a professional career in football were sparked by watching Tottenham's glorious Double team of 1960–61 on television. 'I knew football was what I wanted to do,' he says. 'I wanted people applauding me.' He got that all right . . . but along with the applause came the spit, the bananas flung at him, the abuse.

Graham Adams was the national coach of Bermuda, and he made the arrangements with West Ham for Best to travel to London. He wrote to the club, and they sent back the tickets. Phil Woosnam, who was a former West Ham captain and was now based in North America, had seen Best play and provided an endorsement to the manager.

Greenwood did not need too much convincing and within a matter of weeks Best was welcomed into the first-team squad. 'At 17 years old, I was in the same dressing-room as Bobby Moore, Geoff Hurst and Martin Peters, which was something. They had helped England win the World Cup and now I was among them. But as a soccer player, once your teammates find out that you can play, then the respect you get provides a natural bonding.'

His debut against Arsenal ended in a draw and like your first day at school, while the whole match itself is not vivid, incidents stand out; one in particular.

'Early on I went over the top on Terry Neill and he chased me all over the park.'

Neill, who later became the Arsenal manager, leading them to victory in the 1979 FA Cup final, recalls it too, but he remained a great admirer of Best. He says: 'There are some things in football that you do not forget and to get a bad tackle from a powerhouse like Clyde Best on his debut is something that I did not forget. It was a typical forward's tackle.

'He was a newcomer and to be honest you could tell that he probably could not tackle a fish supper but I can assure you that at the end of the game he understood what the English game was all about. An old-stager like me made sure he was given a welcome to the real world. But I respected him because he was a wonderful player.

'He was 6 ft 2in. but for such a tall, big guy he had a lovely, soft touch of the ball which took us all by surprise; such delicacy when you would least expect it.

'In the 1960s you tended to have two types of forwards: one was the Jimmy Greaves-style player, who would dash around, and work off the centre-forward; the other was the big man, who laid off the passes, very much the front man who combined so well with the nippy guy. That was Clyde.

'Then, when I became a manager and we were facing Clyde, I would ensure my teams knew how to handle him. Centre-halves would normally have tough battles with the big centre-forwards, it was like the collision sometimes of two hammer throwers, but I remember telling the players that they must not let this Clyde Best fool you. He has all that but he does have a neat touch and beware.

'He took a fair bit of abuse and that in a way was inevitable; never from the players, which was important, but I remember at Arsenal I signed a stream of black players, such as David Rocastle, Paul Davis, Raphael Mead and Chris White all as kids and you have to think they were there because of the manner in which Clyde had paved the way for them to be capable of making it in the game and not succumbing to the abuse.

'The fact he sees it now as something that he was able to use to the advantage of others sums up Clyde: a wonderful character who was not just over here for a good time. He was great for the game and what came after it.'

Best used to watch the way Hurst excelled in his role as a target man; the way he moved, the way he allowed the game to work for him and the space he used to create for himself, and he learnt from what he saw. He progressed through a West Ham career where he scored 47 times and represented Bermuda in the qualifying competition for the 1970 World Cup finals.

For Best, his most memorable goal arrived one night during a youth-team game. He takes great pleasure in recalling how he flicked the ball over his head, and that of the defender too, and had spun around in enough time to volley it into the back of the net.

He left West Ham in 1976 for America, and had a spell in their league; then along with his wife Alfreida, he opened up a dry-cleaning business in California. The lure of returning to Bermuda became all the more tempting when he became their national team manager. That ended in 2000, when he took an 18-month sabbatical before applying for a job helping people again: this time, instead of on the football fields, in a prison.

He likes to call himself an eastender because the area means so much to him and, to this day, when he returns to London he goes back to the local people he knew and reminisces about times which at first might have been hostile to him, but which saw him rise through the mist.

'What I always admired about England was the way that history was so important. In 100 years' time, people will still know who Bobby Moore was and who Sir Stanley Matthews was. It will always be that way because tradition in football is something that does not seem to be broken. There is a special feeling about football in England.

'Now I am getting older, I miss that and I miss the east end. Friends there are friends for life; when you go back after years, it is as though you have just returned from a holiday. I say I have – a holiday that has lasted a little bit longer than two weeks!'

He had set down in stone a way forward for the black players and how they emerged. But no player in the 1970s, perhaps ever for England, showed as much potential as Laurie Cunningham, whose skill and speed is still talked about in the east end at Leyton Orient and regularly in the Midlands at West Bromwich Albion, where he produced the football that changed his life. But for him, it was to lead to tragedy.

# 8. The Loss of Laurie Cunningham

THE FIRST BLACK FOOTBALLER TO REPRESENT ENGLAND WAS Laurie Cunningham in April 1977 in a match against Scotland. Just over 12 years later he was dead, killed in a car crash near Madrid in Spain.

It was a high-speed end to a life where speed was essential: his own speed, which terrorised defenders and made him among the best players in the world at the time. But behind the image that Cunningham created with his colourful clothes and love for disco dancing, there was a quiet man who did not seek publicity and was not quite sure how to handle it.

Cunningham had achieved a rare distinction in his career: no other footballer has played for both Manchester United and Real Madrid, arguably the biggest two club sides in the global game. But with just six full England caps, did his talent remain unfulfilled?

Cunningham died on 15 July 1989. I never had the chance to see him live in action, though he was one of the most talented footballers to emerge from the east end of London. His career took off after he was discarded from Arsenal and snapped up by Orient in 1974. As a teenager he drove his first manager to frustration and left his next manager bemused. But whether it was George Petchey, John Giles or Ron Atkinson, they all knew that sometimes eccentricity goes hand-in-hand with class.

The fact that Atkinson compares Cunningham to George Best, perhaps the greatest British player of all time, is surely compliment enough. But his rise to riches and the fame that he hated, and the untimely, tragic death of the winger who had such skill is ultimately a sad tale of a man who did not quite know what he was letting himself in for. When he achieved the success he had been striving for throughout his career, he was not sure if he wanted it after all.

Laurie Cunningham was born in north London in March 1956. After excelling as a youngster he joined Arsenal, with a crop of schoolboy players including Irishman Liam Brady, where the competition has hardly been tougher. He was surplus to requirements and on the same day, both Cunningham and Glenn Roeder were released by Arsenal to Orient, the pair becoming two of the best English players to learn their trade in the east of the capital.

Orient were in the old Second Division, money was tight (when has it not been for the Cinderella club of the east end?) and the name Cunningham had cropped up in talk; Roeder's father was a friend of the Orient manager Petchey.

'Glenn's dad said that if they let Laurie go, you should get hold of him,' recalls Petchey. 'Then someone involved in the Sunday team that Laurie played for actually wrote to me to tell me that Arsenal were not going to take him on and that he needs a lot of help, while at the same time they were saying what a great player he was. I thought: it is about time I took a look at this boy.'

Arthur Rowe had been manager of the renowned Tottenham Hotspur team of the 1950s, dubbed the 'push and run side' for the successful style in which they played the game, and by 1974 his career had taken him to scouting, for Petchey at Orient. A player with West Ham during the Malcolm Allison–Noel Cantwell era, injury had curtailed Petchey's opportunity to gain a regular place in the side at Upton Park and though he played a couple of matches for the first team, he moved to QPR, where he spent eight years. Rowe was manager at Crystal Palace by then and he took Petchey across to this south part of London, where he spent 12 seasons before learning the managerial trade as an assistant at the club. Petchey joined Orient in 1971 as manager and Rowe then began working with him.

One Saturday morning after Cunningham and Roeder had been

brought across Orient had arranged a practice match for some of the young players. It would give the management the chance to have a look at whom they might take on as apprentices for the forthcoming season, and whom they thought had the ability to go all the way.

'I told Arthur to keep a close eye on the outside-right because I kept getting some great reports about him,' says Petchey, chuckling because of the response that was almost immediate. 'I was not watching the start of the game but not long after they kicked off, Arthur walked across to me and told me that I had better get this kid, because he is bloody brilliant. I went to have a look and that afternoon we signed him straightaway. It was amazing . . . his talent was undeniable.'

The youngster who was discarded by Arsenal, and who suffered with depression as a little boy, was built into an England player with a lot of tender care and patience from manager Petchey.

He was a genius on the pitch, a player who would leave teams in England and Europe dazzled with his skill, but often made his managers tear their hair out.

On his first morning as the players were preparing for training, they realised Cunningham had not turned up. A representative from Orient was sent around to his family's house in Islington and the player was there, killing time, unaware that he had to come into the club each day. He was now a professional footballer, but he thought that meant just turning up on a Saturday afternoon or Wednesday evening to play a game.

'When we got there on that first morning and explained to him what was happening, his mother was in tears because she never thought he would even get a job,' says Petchey.

The club's requirements of him had to be spelt out to Cunningham. All he wanted to do was play, not realising the role of apprentices at the club, which included carrying the balls out onto the training pitch, although they did not clean boots.

Once he had arrived and the menial tasks had been completed, Petchey was left in no doubt as to what he had secured. Cunningham was the fastest sprinter in the side; he would also win the longer races, and his touch and speed were immaculate. But he was Laurie – and at first nothing could change his frustrating behaviour.

He was earning around £50 a week and on one of those weeks, he was fined every day for not being there on time and in the end he owed the club money. 'I spoke to him and said it was silly because he was losing out,' says Petchey. He replied that he was always late because no one got him up so Orient ended up by sending their trainer Peter Angell around to his house to wake him each morning. 'It became the in joke. Within a year though, Laurie was first in,' Petchey adds.

Within months, he was catching the eye whenever he played. If Clyde Best had paved the way for the black player to appear on the scene by rights, if not by default, then Cunningham took it to another level. Nobody could fail to be impressed when he received the ball because of what he was capable of doing with it.

When he later moved to West Brom, defender Brendan Batson, the former deputy chief executive of the Professional Footballers' Association, who has now returned to the club as managing director, was a full-back in the same side.

He says: 'Laurie was just so graceful on the ball, he had such wonderful balance, he was so subtle with an explosive shot, tremendous to watch and capable of causing problems on either flank and he had the exquisite movement that you would normally expect to see in a ballet dancer.'

That graceful movement would explain why, as well as playing for Orient, Cunningham earned substantially more money at night appearing on stage in London for a Jamaican dance group.

'I was annoyed at first because he was going to this company and dancing for them,' says Petchey. 'He was a brilliant mover and though I never knew how deeply involved he was with them, I told him he could not put himself at risk of an injury. I said he could not do it after a Wednesday night because of the Saturday game coming up and if we had a midweek match, he could not do it at all. But Laurie was getting about £200, so you could see why he did it.'

It was Cunningham's glorious movement that everyone who watched him used to drool over. Brian Clough was manager of Derby at the time and after an FA Cup third round replay with Orient at the Baseball Ground (the teams had drawn 2–2 at Brisbane Road in the initial match), he made enquiries about signing Cunningham even though the fabulous winger had ended up on the losing side, when Orient were beaten 2–1. That night he had completely stolen the show with his mesmerising speed and ability. Cunningham was sensational. Every trick in his magic box had been taken out: his movement, his skill, his control of a game. If ever a landmark occasion could be pinpointed as to when Laurie Cunningham became one of the most talked-about young talents around, that evening was it.

Petchey told Clough that as Cunningham was only a teenager, he did not want to sell him because he knew there was much more to come from him. He had so much confidence on the ball that he did not have to worry: if he shot on sight, it would rarely be off target, and with his speed he was a very difficult player to catch. Batson recalls how pleased he was to be in the same side as him, watching him go at defenders instead of having to be the man to stop him.

Cunningham had been at Orient for a year when Petchey realised that the best way to allow a talent such as his to evolve was to let his skill grow naturally. All the coaching staff wanted to train Cunningham because he was so good but the manager insisted he was left alone. It did not always work, but in training the player's improvement was visible all the time.

While he had cracked getting in on time for training, Petchey discovered when he arrived at Brisbane Road on a matchday morning one Saturday that Cunningham was still the master of the unexpected – off the pitch as well as on it.

As kick-off time drew closer, Petchey realised Cunningham was not there. Then a telephone call came to inform the club that he would not be there because he had been hit by a train the previous night and was still in hospital. Cunningham had been standing on a platform when a train came rolling in and as he stepped forward, somebody opened the door to get out before it had stopped and it whacked him.

'Did I give him some stick when I went to see him!' says Petchey. 'That was Laurie – he could make you angry. Some managers might not have allowed this to happen, but he was such a talent.'

Orient were a mid-table club in the Second Division but word of Cunningham's brilliance had reached Europe. Hamburg came in with an offer of £70,000 that Orient were ready to take. Petchey knew they could get more for the player and he was reluctant to sell him in the first place, but the club insisted on the books being balanced each year and they wanted to cash in. Petchey wanted £115,000. First Division West Brom were interested, and Petchey took Cunningham up to The Hawthorns to meet their manager, John Giles.

The player was in tears, because he did not want to move from his London base, where it had taken him so long to settle, but with a signing-on fee of £1,000, an offer of the same when he won his first England cap, plus a large increase in wages from what he was earning at Orient, Cunningham was in the big time and agreed to the move.

But Giles, now one of the most respected pundits in the game, a columnist with the *Daily Mail* and a member of the wonderful Leeds team of the 1970s managed by Don Revie, only had Cunningham for 12 games before the manager left West Brom. During that time he quickly discovered all about him.

'Laurie was a tremendously skilful player but I was not totally convinced about him. Orient were short of money and the deal was agreed,' says Giles.

It was the final match of the season. West Brom were playing a local Midlands derby with Aston Villa on a Monday. The team had a light training session to eradicate any stiff joints in the morning; a session for which Cunningham did not turn up.

He had not yet secured a place to live in Birmingham, so he would travel up at the start of the week to stay in a hotel, and head back home to his family in north London at weekends.

Giles recalls: 'After training I rang him at his home in London and he was still there. He said he had not come in because he had to go to the bank for his mother and do some other things. I was not interested; I told him I could not accept that. I had been brought up that you did not miss training at all, it is not right for your teammates to have this happen and his approach was that it was no problem. He was just so casual about it all.

'I don't think he fulfilled his potential. There was no doubt he was an outstanding player: he could pass to people superbly, score goals, excite the crowd who loved him, but had he knuckled down there was no end to what he could have achieved because he was one of the best players I have ever come across.'

Ronnie Allen briefly stepped into the managerial role before Ron Atkinson took charge of a West Brom team that became one of the most exciting to watch in the country. Atkinson recalls the best of Cunningham: 'Laurie was a phenomenal player, one of the finest I have ever worked with. He had a spell at West Brom, albeit for too short a time, when he was as good a player as there was in the country. He was arguably as exciting a player as Bestie himself.

'He had great balance and I used to describe him as being someone who could run on snow without denting it.'

Petchey proved a good judge too. Within months of Cunningham joining Albion, he was selected for England's Under-21 side to play Scotland at Sheffield United's Bramall Lane ground on 27 April 1977, becoming the first black player at any level to be recognised by the country. He had to wait another two years to win his first senior cap, six months after Viv Anderson became the first black player to be honoured at senior level. But his Under-21 debut was just typical Cunningham.

The Under-21 side that night was: Paul Bradshaw, Peter Daniel, David Peach, Steve Simms, Paul Futcher, Gary Owen, Laurie Cunningham, Steve Williams, Keith Bertschin, Peter Reid and Peter Barnes – and one man stole the show. There was a crowd of 9,000 at the game and they were on their feet for long spells, applauding the brilliance of Cunningham, who made a series of dazzling runs.

The match had been arranged to prepare the side for a forthcoming UEFA Under-21 game against Finland and five minutes into the second half, Barnes, the flying winger from Manchester City, sent in a corner that Cunningham met with his head to score the only goal of the game.

Petchey knew a move into a higher echelon would lead to greater recognition for Cunningham. A trio in the West Brom side became known as The Three Degrees: Cyrille Regis, Brendan Batson and Cunningham. During their time together West Brom played such scintillating football that it is still talked about today. They were top of the First Division for a time but a six-week freeze during the winter interrupted their momentum and they never regained it.

One match, on 30 December 1978, they played included a stunning 5–3 victory at Manchester United, where Atkinson later moved to as manager, and he recalls: 'It was one of the best games that West Brom have been involved in and when I was at United, people still talked to me about that match, although we had beaten them. Cunningham and Regis were sensational.'

Batson was another player to have come from the east end, this time the north-east, not too far from the area where David Beckham, and, just before him, Teddy Sheringham were raised. Having spent his early years in the West Indies, Batson had never seen football as a child. His family moved to England in 1962, when Brendan was nine, and they lived in Tilbury in Essex before heading down to Walthamstow two years later. This was Batson's home for the next ten years, until his professional career took him to Cambridge.

'The boys I fell in with at school in Tilbury were all into football and my love of the game grew through that,' says Batson, who knew of Cunningham from the local schoolboy scene.

Funny how an area can have such a strong footballing link. Batson, who was signed as an apprentice by Arsenal, used to play in the Regents Park League, the same set-up that brought Harry Redknapp into the game. He was in the same team as a youngster as Terry Burton, who progressed to become manager of Wimbledon.

'I was spotted by Arsenal as a 13 year old and was invited up to Highbury; even then I did not actually think about what was happening,' he recalls. 'I was being guided along a career path and the penny only dropped when I was about to sign as an apprentice.

'I had been playing in school teams, district sides, county sides. The whole game takes you over. I was an apprentice at Arsenal and areas do that for you, there is this link.'

After a spell at Cambridge, Batson joined Albion and though Regis and Cunningham used to socialise more than him, he remembers clearly one night out. 'Cyrille and Laurie were bachelors so they would go out more on their own together,' says Batson. 'But one evening the three of us were in a bar when suddenly Laurie came over all agitated.

'He said that people were staring at us and he wanted to know why. I told him we were getting a lot of publicity as a team, try not to be so uptight. But he was just very sensitive. It was not aloofness; he was not a natural for the limelight.'

On the pitch that 1978–79 season came the game that transformed Cunningham from one of the best domestic players in Britain to one of the most talked about in Europe.

Albion had been one of the top sides in the First Division the previous year, qualifying for the UEFA Cup competition and progressing well. They reached the quarter-finals, where they were drawn against one of the leading sides in Spain, Valencia, a team who had the Argentine star Mario Kempes, who a few months later became the top scorer in his country when they won the World Cup.

That night Cunningham could do no wrong. He was just sensational as Albion drew 1–1, scoring the equaliser and catching the eye of Real Madrid.

Atkinson says: 'When you talk about a player having the game of his life, Cunningham had several but that match was the one that led to Madrid first taking notice of him.

'Valencia had a superb side but he was phenomenal. It was a great team performance but Laurie stood out. Every time he got the ball, he frightened some tough-tackling defenders to death by just running at them with the ball.'

Batson recalls: 'Laurie was out of this world with some of his play that evening.'

Jeff Farmer, now the Executive Producer for football on ITV, was a senior football reporter on the *Daily Mail* covering that match. 'Laurie was fantastic,' he recalls. 'I remember the home crowd throwing oranges at him as he flew down the wing to try to stop him but they failed in whatever they did.'

Six months later a deal with Real Madrid had been secured at just under one million pounds, and Laurie Cunningham moved to Europe. He made a dream start, scoring on his debut and in that first season the club won the League and the Spanish Cup and Cunningham was proving a pivotal member of the team. It was not to last.

An injury after an innocuous challenge forced him out of the game for a long spell the following season, and necessitated three operations. Such a long period of frustration can destroy a player.

The following season Madrid reached the European Cup final, at the Parc des Princes in Paris on a sultry night in May. Cunningham was brought back for the game; he played well, but they were beaten 1–0 by Liverpool with a goal by their left-back, Alan Kennedy.

It was never the same at Madrid for Cunningham after that. When Petchey went out to see him, he saw a change, not in the way he played, in the man himself. 'He was a god at Real,' recalls Petchey. 'It would be fair to say that he was one of the best players in the world at that time.

'When I was watching him that night, he was demanding the ball, playing so well on such a great stage. He did not do what he always wanted to as he did at Orient, but he was fitting in.

'He did have a good career but he needed better advice from the people he became involved with. He was starting to allow himself to be manipulated and once when I saw him after he had gone to Real Madrid, he had a silver suit on, black and white shoes and a trilby hat. I looked at him and said: "Laurie, what are you doing?" He replied: "Why?" and I said to him: "This top gear is not for you, get back to where you were."'

Cunningham left Madrid in 1983, returning to England, by which time Atkinson was manager at Manchester United. He took him back, but Cunningham played only three games. After his full England debut in 1979, he failed to make an impression at the senior international ranks, his last match being an appearance as a substitute against Romania in a 0–0 draw in a World Cup qualifying game on 29 April 1981, just over four years after his sensational first appearance for the Under-21s.

His frustration grew and his career became a series of stop-off points with clubs in Belgium and France, then a short spell at Leicester before he was taken on by Bobby Gould at Wimbledon in 1988 where he played in their famous 1–0 FA Cup final defeat of Liverpool at Wembley.

Cunningham looked set to be in the team for United against Brighton in the 1984 final, but injury ruled him out. Four years later, he was brought on as a second-half substitute to replace Alan Cork and help Wimbledon secure their greatest triumph.

'When I brought Laurie in it was something new for the lads,' recalls Gould. 'They usually expected a signing to come from the lower divisions so to get Laurie was great. What I remember most about him is the way he used to be so light on his toes when he ran. He never fulfilled his potential, he was of the John Barnes era, of that ilk.'

Cunningham had joined Wimbledon not long before the final and drifted away from the club not long after it, Wembley being his last appearance on such a high-profile football field in England. He went back to Spain, looking to re-create the scene of almost ten years earlier, joining Rayo Vallecano, whom he helped win promotion to the top flight in the Spanish League. That meant the following season he would be able to make an emotional return to Real Madrid. Such a return would have been made for Laurie Cunningham. The gifted player thrived on the way the crowd responded to him and even before the start of the following season, he could not wait for a trip back to Madrid.

But it never came. On the night of 15 July 1989, he was heading home in the early hours when his car crashed and he was fatally injured.

'I had spoken to Laurie about two weeks before he died,' recalls Batson. 'He had problems with his knee and toes and was hoping he would be okay for the new season.

'I learned of his death on the news on the radio and then I received a call from Cyrille Regis. Such a tragedy . . .'

Atkinson looks back and wonders what might have been. 'I remember when Laurie played for England against Switzerland and he became a standing passing player,' he says. 'I asked him afterwards: "Why are you doing that?" He said: "That is what they want me to do in the team." I said: "Laurie, your strength is getting hold of the ball and dribbling past people, you keep doing that."

'If at the start he had been playing for a more fashionable club he might have been recognised more by England; West Brom started to become fashionable but Bryan Robson hardly got capped when he was there, and I often wondered if our players had been with one of the big northern or London clubs they might have received much more recognition.

'Laurie was very unlucky when he went to Spain, injuries caused problems and when he first went to Madrid that held him back for quite a long time. When I brought him back to United, although he had his injuries, it was worth watching him just running in training. He had lost some of his pace by then, the lightning zip he had had gone, but his balance and movement were so graceful.

'He had come back to United on a loan period and the day before the Cup final against Brighton, I had pencilled him in to play, he had a fitness test, and I walked over to him and asked him if he was okay. He did not look very fit when he did his training session and he said "No" and that if he played, he would let the boys down.

'A month before he died, I had been out in Spain, Rayo had just won promotion and along with his president, we went out after going to a game at the Bernabeu [Real Madrid's stadium]. Laurie shook my hands afterwards and said, "I will come back here next year and show them." He never had the chance to fulfil that.

'I was at home on the day he died, I received a phone call from a journalist I think, and I had the job of ringing Cyrille.

'Whatever way Laurie was perceived – he liked a night out – and though he was very extrovert in his dress sense and his appearance sometimes, he was a quiet lad. You could talk to him very quietly and he was serious about his football.'

Cunningham's iconic status has been compared with that of James Dean, the film legend of the 1950s who died in the same manner – the huge talent of both was cut short too soon and their lives left so many questions unanswered.

# 9. This Beckham Kid's Quite Good

## OLD TRAFFORD, MANCHESTER, 7 DECEMBER 1986

'HE REALLY IS A SPECIAL LAD. WHEN THE YOUNGSTERS WERE warming up before the start of the competition he stood out among them all. He has great vision, he has great skill, his dedication reminds me of myself as a youngster and he can go a long way.'

Those were the words of Bobby Charlton, spoken to a crowd assembled in one of the suites in the main stand of the most famous club ground in the land on a Sunday afternoon two weeks before Christmas.

The little boy had just received the best present he could have imagined: a week's trip to Barcelona to train with the Spanish club, meet the players, have a tour around the Nou Camp stadium and tell them of his dream to become a professional footballer.

'My big ambition is to play for Manchester United,' said the boy. 'My hero is Bryan Robson and I want to be like him.'

Charlton smiled, the same fond smile that spreads across his face today when he sees the same boy run out at Old Trafford as the highest-profile football player Britain has ever known. The name of the shy boy with the spiky hair and the proud parents by his side was David Beckham.

It is morning in Manchester and, like he does most days, Charlton pops into the travel agency that he owns. He pauses and reflects on the moment 16 years earlier when he first saw Beckham, the 11-year-old schoolkid from north-east London, win the grand final of Charlton's Soccer Skills competition and earn the trip to Spain.

'It was obvious from then with this kid,' says Charlton, the Manchester United legend, one of their finest players, now a director and a key member of England's 1966 World Cup-winning team. 'You sense it. You know when someone has something special and from his control and balance you knew that he had it. But he also had that desire to be a footballer: you could see that from the times that he came to the school.

'Thousands of players had passed through the school. Some stand out; some stand out more than others. He always enjoyed the competition, he was a lovely lad then, he still is now and his progress has been marvellous.'

The school was started by Charlton in 1978, the product of an idea formed when he saw the way youngsters abroad were playing the game during an international trip, and realised he could help develop talent even more among schoolboys in England. His soccer school was one of the first to be opened, but not with the aim of cultivating youngsters for the big time. 'We wanted people to come and enjoy themselves; it is what football is all about, the basic philosophy of the game,' he says.

Beckham made his name during a week's course at the school, a week's course to break up the summer holiday of a youngster who was football crazy. Soccer schools can be funny places. Some kids go there just for the break from a diet of morning television, others go because their friends are there and some believe it is the start of their careers.

In Manchester, the former City midfielder Mike Summerbee was also running his own soccer school at that time and by 1986 the concept had grown to such an extent that the Bobby Charlton venture would go beyond just a six-week spell during the longest school holiday of the year.

He might not have played for England for 16 years, he might have been retired from the game for almost a decade, but his link with the boys of 1966 has made Charlton one of the greatest ambassadors of the worldwide game.

I remember having the honour of sitting next to Charlton to watch, on television, the draw for the qualifying matches for the 1998 World Cup. I had been invited to a special reception at a sports café bar in London as a reporting assignment and if heaven on earth was possible, this was probably it on that particular afternoon. On my left sat Charlton and on my right sat Pelé, as we watched, along with a handful of others, on a giant video screen when the names were drawn out of the hat.

There is an unwritten rule that journalists do not ask for autographs: it is unethical. You are there to do a job. But on occasions rules are allowed to be broken and that afternoon was the only time in my 20 years in the profession that I have gone against the tide. Pelé, the greatest player in the history of the game, and Charlton, perhaps one of the only 11 men who will ever win the World Cup for England, signed my notepad.

There lay the reason why in 1986, it was difficult to find any extra places on the course; 20 years on from that day at Wembley, the name of Charlton still carried a special meaning, with his schools as packed as ever.

The process was simple. Throughout the year, there would be competitions across the country and those who progressed through the earlier stages would gather together in Manchester for the grand final. If a child could not get a place in the summer, there was no need to worry because representatives from the school would travel the length and breadth of the country holding two-day courses: the winners of these events would be entered into the final. The schools were there to discover which player had the best all-round skill, from the way they could head a ball to the direction they found with a pass.

At the time Bryn Cooper was a physical education teacher in the area and he helped run a Sunday football team called Salford Boys. Bobby Charlton's representatives were travelling around the area to find suitable coaches for the soccer schools to go alongside the football gurus that had already been brought in, such as Tony Whelan, who was with United, Alex Gibson, who was at City, and Dave Bushell, an

England schoolboys coach, who ended up taking the soccer schools on the Isle of Man.

Cooper was excited by the idea and with his friend Ray Whelan from Salford Boys, they met Charlton, discussed the concept and the plan was put forward that Cooper should become the director of football.

Beckham was a youngster playing for a team in the Chingford area of north-east London called Ridgeway Rovers. The previous summer he had been on the course and made little impression. He was back 12 months later, securing a place for the week's stay in Manchester in student accommodation at the university, where the course took place in the vast grounds. It was the final week of the summer programme, week F, and Beckham arrived for duty on the morning of Bank Holiday Monday, 25 August.

There were 292 boys on the course that week and Beckham was assigned registration number 20/033 and selected to be in group 12 of the 18. There were two types of residential students, those who were there for five days or seven, and Beckham was there for the shorter time. There were 15 other boys in his group, all of them 11 years old. Not too many people will know that for one week in his life David Beckham, England captain, international sporting icon and celebrity, actually played for West Germany – the name of his group! The boys were under the stewardship of Mike Madden, a local coach. On the register, there was a mis-spelling of the youngster who was second from bottom on the list: 'David Breckham' eventually had the 'r' crossed out of it, and there could be no doubt of how to say his name or even how to spell it by the time his parents arrived on the Friday to collect their son for the long journey home.

The youngsters had to complete five tasks: long and lofted passing; dribbling; target shooting; touch and juggling; and short passing. The individual scores from each section would be added together and the player with the largest total would be the winner, qualifying for the grand final at Old Trafford.

During the six weeks of the course, the highest any other youngster achieved was 940. Someone scored as low as 540, but the average was between 850–900. David Beckham ended the week with 1,100 points.

Cooper remembers one goal that stood out, with Charlton watching and admiring the skill it took to score. 'We are playing a practice match and the goalkeeper kicked the ball out,' says Cooper. 'The ball was caught by the youngster on the halfway line. He controlled it brilliantly with his foot, lobbed it up in the air and smashed it back over the goalkeeper.

'But it wasn't David who scored it. It was a guy called Jonathan Moyes from Plymouth, who really stood out for me because of his ball skills. At first in the week, David did not catch the eye. But in a way, that shows the quality of the boys we had coming through and David ended up the best of them in that week, against the standards that were being set.'

It did not take too long, though, for his individual skill to come hurtling through. For a boy of 11, he was defying logic with some of the control he had and his passing ability.

'I remember Mike saying what a good kid he had in his group and when he came through with more than 1,000 points, we all stood up and took notice,' recalls Cooper. 'Not many of that age could do anything like that.'

Beckham won the skills competition by 150 points in a week where Liverpool's Craig Johnston, former Manchester United manager Wilf McGuiness, goalkeeper Gary Bailey and skipper Bryan Robson came along as some of the star name guests.

Cooper recalls: 'It was the chance for David to meet his hero, Bryan, who sat for ages just signing autographs for the kids.'

As the week wore on, Cooper could see the skill that the whole world now knows; the player who has such immaculate passing ethics during a game was emerging. He coached him in the evening five-a-side competitions, when Beckham played in a team then called Bobby Charlton's Dazzlers. 'He was always working, he had non-stop energy and if he was ever knocked over, he would just get straight up again, think nothing of it because he was so determined to keep going,' recalls Cooper. Even at lunchtime, when the youngsters would congregate to eat, Beckham and a handful of others would often be outside the dining room . . . playing more football.

Once the five-a-side sessions were finished, the boys would be taken to bowling and have a series of other competitions to test their sporting ability: from pool to boardgames to table tennis to Subbuteo. Beckham never won any of those, and if the clock is rolled forward 16 years to Friday, 7 June 2002, few people in Britain must have been less confident than Cooper when the England captain stepped up to the spot in Sapporo to take the penalty against Argentina in the group stages of the World Cup finals. For during his time at the Bobby Charlton soccer skills week, his penalty taking was awful. There used to be competitions every day and Beckham never once progressed, missing more than he scored.

He made up for it with his overall ball control. Cooper remembers: 'He had such wonderful skill and vision even then. He was way above the ability of the boys of his age, and even higher age groups, with his dribbling, his shooting and the way he would chip the ball forward.'

He came back two years later, when he was 13; this time he was put in an age group with teenagers of 16 and 17 and still beat them all, scoring 900 points but not winning the overall competition this time.

But he had done enough to confirm his reputation, because in the summer 1986, it may have been the final week but Beckham was on his way to the grand final in the first weekend of December.

The first day in a new job is always a bit daunting and though I had been working on the newspaper for a year, I had stepped into the hot seat as sports editor of the *Waltham Forest Guardian* in north-east London. To receive a telephone call about going to Old Trafford was the best medicine to calm the nerves: what a week it was going to be.

It meant that, being the local reporter following David Beckham, I had to watch his every move and on that Sunday, my scrutiny of the now most-scrutinised player in the world was easy. In a mass of boys, all wearing white shirts, black shorts and black socks, he stood out because his football was immaculate.

At just over 11, he ran away with the competition. It had been a spectacular weekend for the youngsters and their families. While some of them had ambitions to become footballers, they were making the most of what for the majority of them was a once-in-a-lifetime occasion.

I remember standing with Beckham's parents, Sandra and Ted, during the indoor event. They stressed how much David wanted to be a footballer; he did nothing else, just played as much as he could with every spare moment he had after school. Yet I have always thought that if I had asked any of the parents the same thing that day, they would all have probably come up with the same answer. Time has shown that whatever Beckham did all those years after school, his ability and desire took him to where he wanted to be.

In part, that great ability could be seen that Sunday afternoon in Manchester. The finalists had come from across the country and one of them, Darren Hargreaves, who now works as a joiner in Bolton, remembers how even then Beckham stood out, though says you would not have noticed it on the bus that took the boys to the event. Hargreaves was 14, and having qualified himself with a high score, he sat on the back row of the bus.

'David was just in front of me and we were all quite quiet,' he says. 'I suppose nerves do set in when you are involved in something like that.

'I always remember though that as much as he was a lot younger than me, he was an extremely skilful player and a very good footballer.

'There was this target that we had to hit, about 30 to 40 yards away, aiming for a cone that was in the middle and he kept knocking it over. It is not surprising he passes the ball the way he does today because the way he would use it then was fantastic – and he was only 11.'

The seed had been planted in the young Beckham's mind that one day he wanted to be back here doing the same, but in a United shirt, preferably that of his hero Robson. What was amazing about him that day was his confidence; he was in with boys who were older than him, some by seven years, but give David Beckham a ball and he could do no wrong.

The official hotel for the tournament was the Piccadilly in Manchester, not far from the station, and the boys were asked to check in by early evening on the Saturday. Parents were invited and the competition began on the Sunday morning. First stop was Manchester United's training ground for the first three rounds of the event indoors: ball juggling, target shooting and short passing. Typically, Beckham was in front from the start, gaining extra points in the opening discipline, where the ball had to be dropped from the player's hands onto the floor and before it bounced a second time, the juggling had to start.

He increased his early lead in the competition by taking advantage of the bonus system with ten points given every time a player used a part of the body other than their feet: his control was superb, from his head, to his chest, and what was clearly visible was his balance, and the way he had control of the ball with both feet. Not only did Beckham manage to keep the ball in the air for the maximum of a minute to earn 200 points, the bonuses flew in with all the trickery he used.

He was never overtaken in the competition, stretching his lead in the next discipline, the target shooting, where different points were scored for what corner and what height the ball reached when driven into an empty goal and then in the final event of the first phase, the short passing, he again excelled with both feet: looking as good with his left as his right.

At lunchtime the boys were taken to Old Trafford, before the competition resumed at 2.00 p.m. on the pitch itself. The youngster, who had been attracting the close attention of Spurs, the nearest professional side to his north London home, had always put Manchester United at the top of his list of clubs and now he was going to experience playing on his field of dreams . . . the Old Trafford turf.

When they announced the final result on the pitch, it came in front of a crowd of more than 40,000 fans because the schedule had been set so that the winner would be paraded before the teams came out for Manchester United's First Division game with Tottenham, a match that was being shown live on television late that afternoon. Football can provide such ironies; the crowd chanted Beckham's name and cheered when they learnt he was a Manchester United fan. They were not too happy when they discovered he was from London, and so near to Tottenham, but it was jovial enough. Although they did not realise it, the fans were treated to a glimpse of the future for a brief half-hour, when the 48 finalists came out onto the pitch to complete the last two disciplines of the event, dribbling and long passing.

Beckham summed up his feelings afterwards when he said: 'It was such a fantastic thrill to play out there. It has been a dream. I hadn't been able to eat for two days but I am pleased.'

The dribbling contest lasted 30 seconds for every player: they had to run in and out of eight cones, and then run to the far cone with the ball and back again. Beckham, typically, achieved additional points for being inside the time limit without putting a foot wrong. The long passing could have been made for him: a target had been set, as it was in the week in Manchester that had brought him to this moment, and players had to hit three different areas depending on their age group.

Beckham's passing landed further than it should have done for his age, to win him more points and the cheers of a growing crowd arriving for the big match; he also hit a cone directly, which brought an extra 100 points.

Whenever I watch a United game at Old Trafford and Beckham, now in all his glory, launches a ball forward for Ruud Van Nistelrooy to chase or heads off on a dazzling run down the wing, I think back to that cold afternoon in December 1986.

The vision of the future was making his mark and he won the competition in typical Beckham style, scoring 1,110 points overall, 10 more than he had achieved on his record week back in August.

The year before the competition had been won by Vietnam's Hung Wang, who then went on to the National School of Excellence at Lilleshall before being signed on schoolboy terms by Tottenham. He treated the Old Trafford crowd with a display of his tricks before Beckham was handed his award.

'It was only a week's course and look at the great rewards it has brought us,' said his father, Ted, whose first name is actually also David.

It was ironic that on the same day he was winning this competition in such spectacular style, back home in north-east London another record was being broken by Ridgeway Rovers, the Sunday team that he played for.

The Under-12s won 4–1 at Enfield Rangers and in the process scored the 1000th goal in the club's history, a history that had seen Beckham convert many of those himself. On that day, Micah Hyde and Jason Brissett were both on target, the two of them progressing to professional careers, now at Watford and Leyton Orient respectively.

At Old Trafford, the one-boy show had come to an end, for now at least, and United knew that this was not going to be the last time they would see him in action. He had too much confidence to allow what he had achieved that afternoon to slip away from him. He cherished the picture he had taken with Charlton.

You could not have made it up for Beckham, who then sat down to watch a tremendous First Division game between Manchester United and Spurs that ended 3–3 before heading back home to more acclaim.

But if winning in front of a large crowd was a dream for Beckham, it was just the beginning. His prize took him to Spain the following May, where he trained with a Barcelona team that was managed by Terry Venables and included Gary Lineker, Mark Hughes and Nayim.

The name of Beckham was growing in football circles because he had been such a phenomenon at Old Trafford that Sunday. United ensured they paid close attention to his moves. Clubs from across London and the rest of the country watched him, but on 2 May 1989, his 14th birthday, he was signed by Alex Ferguson on schoolboy terms, a contract that would begin the following September with him moving to Manchester.

'It didn't take too long to decide,' said Beckham. 'I have always supported Manchester United and the people there are so friendly.

When I went up there to sign, Bryan Robson came up to wish me good luck. I told him I was after his shirt.'

He got more than that; he gained his captain's armband, at both club and international level and became the most famous United player since the days when George Best took the image of the game beyond a mere 90 minutes on a Saturday afternoon.

But it could have been so different. The darling of Old Trafford, David Robert Joseph Beckham, may never have pulled on a red shirt at all . . .

## 10. Letting Go of Beckham

FOOTBALL WAS ALWAYS DAVID BECKHAM'S NUMBER ONE
ambition. He wanted to do nothing else, and in every spare moment
he would be practising, whether it was in the garden with his mother,
or at the park nearest to his house in Chingford. The small youngster
with the blond hair was constantly trying to improve his technique.

But, like most teenagers, he wanted to earn some extra pocket
money and though football has now made him the richest player in
England with salary and endorsements, back in 1988 £3 an hour was
enough. It is estimated that he earns that amount every 18 seconds
since signing a new contract at Manchester United worth a reported
£100,000 a week, but when Beckham was 13, he took a job less than
a mile from his home in Chingford.

Four nights a week, the greyhound stadium in Walthamstow is
packed with racing enthusiasts and in their Paddock Grill Restaurant,
the boy who was destined to become the most famous football player
on the planet was happy to be a dogsbody. His friend at Chingford
High School, William Kincaid, was already working in the restaurant
and through him, Beckham was taken on. For the six months that
Beckham was there, restaurant manager Valentine Yerrall remembers
him being totally obsessed with football.

'I was just grateful that the glasses that David had to collect were
not made of rubber because he would probably have kicked them all
the way back to the kitchens,' says the now-retired Yerrall. 'He had a
"dogsbody" role because we needed pot-boys; David was only with us
for about six months but he would do anything we wanted him to do

. . . he was always talking about football. He knew then what he wanted to be and there is no surprise that he made it because he had so much ambition.'

That ambition had surfaced when Beckham was as young as seven. At that age he answered an advert in his local paper for players. A new team called Ridgeway Rovers had just formed and they were looking to build up their young side.

On a Sunday morning in the summer of 1982, Beckham turned up as requested in Chase Lane Park in Chingford for a team that was managed by Stuart Underwood and coached by Steve Kirby, a carpenter by trade but who had been with Tottenham as a youngster in the same era as Graeme Souness and Jimmy Neighbour. Kirby had not made it in the professional game but he was determined to keep his hand in at football as much as he could. He thrived on the challenge of training the youngsters at Ridgeway, but such was the crop of talent, that even at seven, they did not need too much instruction.

Three other youngsters in the team, Chris Day, now at QPR, and as mentioned, Micah Hyde and Jason Brissett, progressed into the professional game. Kirby's son, Ryan, was a trainee at Arsenal, before going to Doncaster, Crewe, Wigan and Northampton and then into the non-league scene, where he has been captain of Aldershot.

Beckham stood out for a number of reasons, including his blond hair and his size.

His height was the big, or should it be small, problem: he was the tiniest player in the team. Perhaps Beckham's attitude today on the pitch, and the way he has turned his game around after being sent off at the World Cup finals in France in 1998 for that petulant and unnecessary kick on Diego Simeone, is linked to the way he learnt to handle himself as a youngster when all was not going his way.

Kirby says: 'He has a stronger personality than I would have given him credit for. How he dealt with the stuff with the sending off was exceptional.

'As a youngster, the opposition always tried to kick him because being blond and not too tall, they thought he was this little flash kid and he was there for the taking. They could not have been more wrong. He was small but give him a ball, and even at that age, he was a great influence. He could kick it so well, he would time it lovely, strike it superbly and though he was not very big, the skill and enthusiasm of this blond kid made up for that.

'I would never have thought he would have grown like he has now. But with David there is a difference. Joe Cole [of West Ham] was fantastic as a schoolboy but I can't see him ever having the presence of David.

'You are not going to tell me that when Pelé was eight, people thought he would become what he did, but some kids can play and David was one of those from the first moment I set eyes upon him. You can tell: with David, he might not have had the height but he had the body shape and skills.'

In the seven years that Beckham spent at Ridgeway, the team became the best boys side in the area, at one stage playing more than 100 games without defeat: he scored over 200 goals and the team won every competition they played. Ridgeway were unbeatable in the Enfield and District League, winning the title for three years in a row; then they moved to a stronger league in the area and they won that too, along with County and London cups. And they stayed together. Normally as youngsters grow up, they drift in and out of football but from when the Ridgeway side was formed, they remained as one. During that time, not only did the side itself rarely change, but they lost just two players.

Each year they would arrange to compete in a European tournament and one summer they travelled to Holland for a competition with mixed age groups. The majority of teams were older than the Ridgeway boys, who were nine. They were in the same event as ten year olds, but, unaware of their talents, the organisers actually made the pitches smaller so the younger boys would not be worn out: the opposition might as well have gone home then.

Goalkicks were allowed to be taken from the edge of the penalty area and it was an opportunity for Beckham just to shoot. 'It was amazing,' recalls Kirby. 'I do not think they realised what we had in players such as David and all the others.'

With endless goals, Ridgeway strolled to victory in that tournament. It was becoming the norm: the side had such a good collection of players that they were proving too good for any team put in front of them.

Then they entered a tournament called the Norwich Cup, arranged by the football club from Carrow Road, and when they played their first match, their next opponents, a team from Glasgow, were watching, thinking they had worked out a way to stop the side's key player: Beckham. As the game started, they began to kick him. And they did so around the edge of the box.

Whatever the age group, from a seven-year-old goalkeeper flapping at a shot on a Sunday park to a stunned Greek goalkeeper watching the ball fly past him, there has always been no stopping the lethal free kicks that have become the Beckham trademark. 'They did not realise that if you give away a free kick in those positions, he will score,' says Kirby of the game that Ridgeway won 2–0.

Norwich were managed at the time by Ken Brown, who after the tournament spoke to the Ridgeway officials about the players. 'But we knew David was being watched by Manchester, even then,' says Kirby.

Next stop was another tournament, this time in Ipswich, where they were matched against an England Schoolboy side consisting of youngsters who were two years older than the Ridgeway boys.

'Beforehand it might have looked like it would be a one-sided game,' says Kirby. 'But they just managed to beat us 3–2, it was good fun, a bit of a challenge and do not forget that they were just a club team'.

While Beckham was blessed with natural talent, and worked hard after school and in every spare moment he had to improve upon it, he still had to be taught. Training with Underwood and Kirby was not always an evening of admiring the talent on show.

Kirby says: 'There was much you had to tell David and hope it would eventually go in. 'When you have naturally gifted players, they tend to do stuff you can't coach anyway; the manner of their control and the approach they have to a game. What you have to do is tell them what they must not do, such as try to be too clever inside their penalty box.'

What is it about David Beckham and penalties? Ridgeway were playing in the County Cup and as Beckham strode up, he fired the spot kick over the bar. 'It just sticks in my mind,' says Kirby. But the amount of victories they had was endless.

Kirby was training the YTS players at Wimbledon at the time that the Ridgeway youngsters were becoming a formidable force, with the skill of Beckham and the goalscoring of Hyde. 'They were so good at the ages of seven and eight, the training you could do with them was what I would do with the YTS boys or even men in terms of their skill levels. From ball control to passing to heading to practice matches, they were such a wonderfully talented group.'

With Manchester United posters on his wall, Bryan Robson as his hero and a desire to play for the biggest club team in England, Beckham had just one ambition. But that team could easily have been Spurs, his local club, and where would the Beckham story be today if it had?

Len Cheesewright is one of the game's legendary scouts. He refuses to reveal how old he is but does not deny that he is at least 83. He has just left Orient, having discovered players that range from Roeder to Sol Campbell. As a tribute to Cheesewright, an east Londoner who has been involved in more than 300 transfer deals, Roeder took his West Ham side back to Orient in the summer for a testimonial match for the man who brought him into the game. In 1988, he was working at Spurs under Terry Venables and knew the Beckham family well.

Cheesewright would be the classic embodiment of a scout. Wherever there was a game and the possibility of spotting new talent, he would be there. Hackney Marshes on Saturdays and Sundays were his regular haunts. Beckham played there in cup matches for Ridgeway and Cheesewright first saw him play when he was 12.

'He could not win a ball to save his life and he used to get knocked off the ball,' he says. 'But what he could do better than anyone else I had ever seen at that age was take a free kick or a corner. He was a little boy but with his corners, he could reach the far post with his efforts, they were amazing, so full of power and strength.

'He has not improved today – because he was so good then. When he took a corner, it was a goal. If he took a free kick a long way out, it would hang in the air and even a bloke who could not play would put it in.

'Depending on the position you are looking at, I always looked for a player who had ability, whether they were stronger than someone else, if they were an intelligent player and if they stood out as soon as they touch the ball. Beckham had that ability.'

But the battle to sign the player was growing. His father was being bombarded with interest for Beckham and a deal for schoolboy terms with Tottenham looked to be the way forward: it was a London club, would be a secure start and was only about three miles from his Chingford home.

Cheesewright takes up the story.

'We were going to sign him and we missed him by a couple of minutes,' he says. 'I arrived at Spurs' ground on the night that it was all going to happen, the night we were going to secure him on schoolboy terms. We had a pressroom at the top of the main stand and he was there with his mother and father.

'We all headed upstairs and I had schoolboy forms ready. Any problems had been swept away and his mother particularly did not want him to go to Manchester United because it was too far away from home; that was only a natural reaction from a parent.

'He sat down at the desk and we were about to agree on the deal that was about to be signed when his father got wind of a rumour that there were people at the club who thought he was too small. I expected the deal to be completed when suddenly his dad stood up and said: "Sorry, Len, we are away."

'He had heard something about some people at the club who did not believe he was big enough and thought that might affect him on his way in his career. But it probably meant that Spurs lost out on that day to the player who has become the best footballer in England and the biggest name in the game in the world.

'Just imagine what the outcome would have been had the club had the luck to have signed Beckham. They had Sol Campbell too and Spurs would have cracked it down south. What are they worth now on the transfer market? I don't think you could even put a figure on it; thinking about it is hard enough.

'David spent quite a long time at Spurs, he had been around at one or two clubs but he was coming to us regularly. There used to be other scouts around but they did not know they were not in the running. They would come up to me and say we have him tied up.

'It remains one of the biggest mistakes in football because I am sure Beckham would have signed that day. But his father was not silly. If he heard that someone had said he was not big enough, then he made up his mind. The boy was guided by his mother and father and they knew he could go to Manchester United.

'Of course, you regret not signing Beckham but you do not make a song and a dance about it then because no one knows how he is going to turn out. No one could ever have imagined that he would have ended up like he is.'

Where he is now is Britain's most marketable sporting product. His rise to fame has been nothing short of a fairytale, the boy who used to collect glasses in a dog stadium becoming a player who followed the lead of Billy Wright and Bobby Moore, as blond-haired men who became captains of their country. Beckham's hair may still be blond – it changes often enough. His image, at whatever level, is huge; but never once has he lost the consistency that made him such a wanted youngster when at Ridgeway.

Despite all the trappings of fame, he has not changed. He is among the richest sportsmen in the world, but his parents' home remains a small terraced house in Hampton Road and no matter the amount of cars he drives, he has not lost the down-to-earth approach that he had on the first day he arrived for those trials at the park in Chase Lane.

As a senior professional he first came to prominence in the semi-final of the FA Cup in 1994 when Manchester United beat Chelsea 2–1 at Villa Park, Beckham scoring the winning goal. His name was splashed across the back pages and the telephone at his home the following morning never stopped ringing with requests for interviews from television and newspaper journalists. I was there talking to his dad at the time. Beckham Snr had all the newspapers spread across the floor like it was a carpet of print; he had read every word proudly and was going to add them all to the cuttings book. 'This is probably just the start,' I remember telling him. 'We will see,' was his reply. It always sticks with me, because in fact it was the beginning of an incredible career.

Alex Ferguson had played it perfectly, nurturing Beckham through the youth system at United and sending him to Preston on loan to experience life in the professional game. It was while playing a match for Manchester United in 1996 that he made his mark in the Premiership. The country really stood up and took notice as Beckham scored with the wondrous shot that flew in from the halfway line over the head of Wimbledon goalkeeper Neil Sullivan at Selhurst Park. For audacity, it was beyond what a 21 year old should do, but Beckham has never kept to the script.

He made his England debut against Moldova on 10 September 1997 in a game that England won 4–0 at Wembley, the sort of start that eased him into an international career where he is now the first name on the manager's team sheet. He reached the pinnacle of England duty by being made captain for the first time by caretaker managers Peter Taylor and Steve McClaren on 8 November 2000, against Italy.

When Sven-Goran Eriksson took over as the manager of the national team, Beckham was confirmed as his skipper, a role he took into the World Cup finals in Japan in 2002 as England reached the quarter-finals.

He is the most recognisable football face today and his fame has spread beyond that of the game: he was the first man to appear on the front of the women's magazine *Marie Claire*. But as Kirby, the coach who helped bring him through to where he is now, discovered, Beckham has the ability not to let fame take over his life. Kirby was out shopping in Hertfordshire with his wife in a Marks & Spencers store when they spotted a guy with a basket in his hand.

'He was the biggest name in football by now, he had just had his hair cropped, he was instantly recognisable and when we reached the checkout, I asked him if he had enough money to pay!' he says. 'Twenty minutes later, he was still talking to us, signing as many autographs as needed, in no hurry to rush away and he was the same kid from all those years ago. He wanted to know how my children were and in a strange way, it was like he was seeing an old schoolteacher again because he was showing us the same respect he always did.

'Let's be honest, he is a brave boy to have gone to Manchester in the first place; it was quite a step, something that others might not have been able to do. I know it is Manchester United and all that but a young teenager to have to leave his family is asking something.

'David was a family boy, he was not even streetwise, so for him to go up there is something that has to be admired.'

He has never been more admired than when England reached the finals of the 2002 World Cup with his last-minute goal to ensure a 2–2 draw against Greece at Old Trafford, and qualification. It was perhaps his best game for England. He did not stop running, but with the team trailing 1–0, England equalised with a goal created by him and scored by another striker from London's north-east, Teddy Sheringham. He and Beckham were virtually neighbours . . .

## 11. The Teddy and Sol Show

AT NOTTINGHAM FOREST, BRIAN CLOUGH, THE MOST CAPTIVATING club manager of his generation, had a rule about the new striker he had signed from Millwall at the start of the 1991 season. He might have been known as Teddy to his teammates, fans and supporters of his former club, but Clough's new forward had been christened Edward and that was the way it was going to stay for the manager. This might have seemed one of the eccentricities of Clough at the height of his power, but in fact it did not bother the player too much: Edward Paul Sheringham had enough of the money and trappings of football fame not to allow something such as that to give him sleepless nights.

When he was making his mark in the game, he had not been known as Teddy anyway. George Graham nurtured him, Clough sharpened him up and Terry Venables put the finishing touches to a player who would score on a regular basis but was never seen as the linchpin of a side until the European Championships in England in 1996.

Venables was the England coach, and having signed him when he was manager at Spurs as the replacement for Gary Lineker in the summer of 1993, he decided to play him in a deep role behind the attack. It transformed the side and brought out in Sheringham a style that he had always had, but which had never been in such demand before.

He suddenly became the key to England's progress towards the semi-final, never more so than in the 4–1 victory over Holland, a platform which eventually earned Sheringham a surprise move to Manchester United.

When United won the European Cup on that extraordinary night in Barcelona in 1999, not only did Sheringham score the equaliser against Bayern Munich but he flicked the ball on for the winner from Ole Gunnar Solskjaer, ensuring cult status forever at Old Trafford. He was in the right place at the right time, just as he was on 8 October 2001, when Sven-Goran Eriksson ordered him off the bench with England trailing Greece 1–0 in a World Cup qualifier they could not afford to lose.

With his first touch he equalised, heading in from David Beckham's free kick. The cheers were loud enough in Old Trafford that day, but perhaps a north-east corner of London had the rightful claim to that moment.

Nine years Beckham's senior, Sheringham came from Highams Park, a small suburb that sits on the borders of east London and Essex near to Chingford, Beckham's childhood home. It is where the Edward Sheringham story started and no matter the speed of his Porsche, the glamour of his girlfriend or the size of his bank balance, he has not forgotten his roots. Fame to him has been a means to an end: an end that has seen him go back to Tottenham for the third time in his career.

He is now in the team managed by Glenn Hoddle – his boyhood hero – after joining in June 2001 and had also been there previously in 1992 under Venables. Earlier still Sheringham had been with the club in 1980, though that spell did not last long.

As a teenager Sheringham had trials both at Tottenham and Leyton Orient, but neither club took him on. Despite being a regular goalscorer at school and club level, he was never considered good enough to make the professional grade.

His first love was Tottenham, and if Sheringham pursues a route into management, it would be no surprise to see him in charge of Spurs one day; they were his team and that is the way it has stayed. In north-east London in the mid-1970s, the school system was broken into three: junior, junior high and senior. It was when Sheringham, then 14, arrived at the senior level, at St George Monoux in

Walthamstow after attending Selwyn and Chapel End schools, that his football skill could be seen by all. No one ever considered calling him Teddy then; his name was Eddie.

Academically, he was not the greatest of pupils, because all he wanted to do was play football; even the rejections by Spurs and Orient did not lessen his desire to play the game professionally.

In the George Monoux school team Sheringham was consistent, if not spectacular, in a forward partnership with Stephen Bray. The pair helped the school to success and at that time you would not have been able to guess which of them would make it into the professional game, and which would eventually become a trader at Walthamstow Market. Both were confident in their manner on and off the pitch and the majority of times that the ball found its way into the penalty box, one of them would score.

Sheringham attended St George Monoux School between the ages of 14 and 16. His name was known in the area because of his footballing ability; he was the star of teams because of his knack of scoring goals, a skill that Ferguson and Eriksson have discovered on the most important of occasions.

When a child wants to be a footballer, it is often overlooked by schoolteachers who focus on the need for a 'proper' education, but there was no disputing the fact that Sheringham's best subject at George Monoux was putting the ball in the back of the net. He could score from all angles and from long range, and it was an exciting school team to play in. Bray was just as good a footballer.

Bray often talks of the times when Sheringham and he would combine to take another opposing school team to task, but they went their separate ways when they left George Monoux and lost contact. Then, one sunny summer morning, Bray was heading to his market stall and stopped at a set of traffic lights en route. He was driving a Hillman Hunter that had seen better days. Whatever song he was listening to on the radio was suddenly drowned out by a booming noise that grew louder by the second.

A car pulled up on his right, a black Porsche with blacked-out windows. Bray turned away, and then looked again as the passenger window came down. Inside was a driver with no shirt on, a tan and a gold chain, who suddenly peered across from under his sunglasses. It was Sheringham and the pair had not seen each other since they left school. Sheringham looked at his old friend, from Porsche to Hillman, and said: 'You flash bastard!' and drove away as the lights changed.

It was typical of Sheringham, who has never hidden the wealth that football has brought him while at the same time remaining a footballer who has not forgotten where his roots are. It could all have been so different for the youngster who would go to school with his colours pinned to his chest, or at least around his neck in the form of a scarf with Glenn Hoddle's name on it that he rarely left off.

Sheringham wanted nothing else but to play football. After his rejections by Spurs and Orient, the non-league scene beckoned and he turned his attentions to one of the area's top sides, Leytonstone-Ilford. They were based at a small ground behind a station and Sheringham, at 16, was poised to become their new striker as, for now, the professional game was proving out of his reach. He played for their youth team until suddenly Millwall, managed by George Graham, came in for him, and his life changed.

As his dad's pet name for him had been Teddy, the football world was introduced to the latest striker from the east of the capital who would play a significant role in the future of the national team under that name.

Teddy signed for Millwall as an apprentice in 1983 and made his first-team debut a year later. After a loan spell at Aldershot, he returned to south London, where he began to establish himself as a regular in the first team.

By the time he left the club to join Nottingham Forest in 1991, he had broken a stack of records. With 93 goals during his time at The Den, he remains Millwall's greatest scorer. There was no better season than the 1987–88 term when his partnership with Tony Cascarino brought 42 goals and took Millwall into the old First Division for the first time in their history. Sheringham was playing from the deep position that has now become his trademark – but not until he emerged in such a role for England in 1996 did his value on the international scene become apparent.

George Graham had saved his career; he might never have been picked up by a professional club if Millwall had not come in for him, and he could have ended up like so many talented footballers out there, who may have the skill but are never given the proper stage to display it.

His spell at Forest lasted two seasons and as Lineker headed to Japan and then retirement in the summer of 1993, Sheringham's name was linked with Spurs. Sheringham was confidence personified when he drove into Tottenham's training ground in Mill Hill one Thursday afternoon to discuss the move with Venables. It was just after 1 p.m. and the manager had finished his usual weekly press conference when the gaggle of reporters and photographers were just leaving. Speculation had been growing over Sheringham, but even the denials were being denied. Then the picture became clear when the player's Porsche swung into the car park.

A deal had not been finalised, yet Sheringham was happy to sit on the bonnet of his car and pose for pictures. Five long hours later, the transfer was completed. Thirteen years before Spurs had said 'No,' but this time they were welcoming him with open arms. By 1997 Sheringham, then 31, was determined his career would not end without a major trophy and talked of his desire for the honours that had not materialised at Spurs. Manchester United came to his rescue.

He was fast gaining a reputation as the man to fill crucial boots; he had succeeded at Spurs as a replacement for Lineker and now, as United looked for a new hero after the departure of Eric Cantona, Sheringham had another challenge ahead of him. In 1999, he could do no wrong as United won the Treble, scoring in the FA Cup final defeat of Newcastle and playing a magical role in Barcelona. It was his intelligence with the ball, his ability to be in the right place and read the play before the script had been written that made Sheringham such an asset.

In the 2000–01 season he was named the Professional Footballers' Association and Football Writers' Player of the Year. While at school, he was determined to make everything he did on the pitch spectacular, but Graham taught him that the simple goal is just as effective and it allowed Sheringham to pursue a new line of attack.

He has fast become the best all-round player in the English game, but perhaps it has happened too late. Time is not on his side, as was shown at the World Cup finals in Japan when he appeared only from the bench.

He always played golf on a public course in Chingford; it was ironic because the rule was that you had to wear red; for a Spurs fan, there could be no worse dilemma. He would then go into the Willow Café near the course after his game, and now he can regularly be seen queuing for a table at one of the most popular restaurants nearby in Woodford. It is just along from the pub where Beckham and Victoria Adams had their first date, a restaurant that you cannot book and sometimes have to wait outside for an hour before there is a free table. But Sheringham insists on no special treatment when he is there with his son Charlie, and he is always happy to sign autographs once inside.

He does not play on his fame: he is just Edward Paul Sheringham, the boy who never gave up when the rejections came in, and his determination has ultimately turned him into one of the most successful sons to have emerged from the east of London.

Amid the euphoria of that goal against Greece, he was mobbed by Beckham and, among others, Sol Campbell, a player born just a few miles away in Newham, discovered on a school pitch by Len Cheesewright, the man who almost took Beckham to Spurs. Campbell has now become a rock in the England defence. Cheesewright, who has handled so many of the top schoolboy players, enabling them to move to clubs in London, lives close to Campbell's family.

Campbell was the only Englishman to be selected in the official World Cup squad by FIFA at the end of the 2002 tournament, following a season where he had moved from Spurs to Arsenal – again, much like Sheringham, to search for honours which came instantly with the Premiership and FA Cup Double. He suffered some of the worst abuse directed towards one player from the team he had just left. But Campbell has never been one to make a fuss. Since the day he was first spotted playing for Rippleway Newham at the Terrence McMillan Stadium near West Ham, he was singleminded about what he wanted to do.

Along with the south London-born Rio Ferdinand, Campbell has become an integral part of the England defence, a key to the Arsenal side and a player who was always more versatile than many of the other youngsters who would pass through Cheesewright's hands.

Cheesewright, then chief scout at White Hart Lane, brought him to the club in 1988. At first Spurs were not sure about his overall quality. He would train at night after school and Cheesewright reveals: 'I knew there was something there because he was talented but the people at Tottenham who ran the youth structure were not sure. I had to persuade them that they should forget about having their doubts.

'Look at where he has ended up . . . it does not surprise me because he had so much commitment.'

Campbell has an amazing ability not to be fazed by things: his calmness is one of his major qualities. On the day he was called up to the England squad, 6 February 1995, the first he knew about it was when he woke up. Spurs had beaten Blackburn the night before and, when I spoke to him that day, he said: 'I'd slept in late and thought I'd better listen to see if there were any messages on the answerphone.' Gerry Francis, then the Spurs manager, had left one. 'I heard his voice and wondered what he wanted before he said, "You've been called up for England."'

He was in Venables' squad for a match against the Republic of Ireland but his debut did not come until a year later when he came on in the 3–0 home defeat of Hungary in the warm-up to the European Championships.

Campbell, at 21, was making a superb impression, having been given his debut at Tottenham by Venables in 1993. But it was

Venables' successor, Ossie Ardiles, who was quick to realise the talent of the player. He said: 'Sol is so versatile. He has played right-back and left-back for us and about the only position he had not played in is in goal. He is the type of youngster who can play anywhere.'

Campbell had always wanted to be an electrician. His first priority was financial stability. He recalled: 'It was important to have a steady job. Being an electrician would have fitted the bill. There was also a time I thought about computing but football is proving the right choice. It is funny how things work out, though, because sometimes I look at where I have progressed to and wonder what would have happened if it had been different.'

But Cheesewright was determined not to let this player slip from his grasp. He helped arrange his place at the National School of Excellence in Lilleshall and remembers going up there one day soon after he started to see Campbell playing on the right. 'Without telling them their job, I suggested that he was perhaps best at the back,' says Cheesewright, who has created a remarkable tradition across London. Roeder chose the final West Ham programme notes of last season to pay tribute to the scout who discovered him.

Cheesewright has lost count of the number of transfer dealings he has been involved in. 'It is more than 300,' he says, 'It must be a world record.' One of his biggest discoveries, if not the biggest, is the player who has the name Sulzeer on his birth certificate.

With West Ham being so close to where he lived, they were the club that Sol wanted to be a part of. He said: 'When I was 13 or 14 I played with the Hammers. But it did not work out and I went back to playing for my district side. Spurs came in for me and it has all progressed from there.'

When he first made his mark at Spurs, he cited Pelé and Paul Ince as his footballing heroes; the latter was, like him, a player who progressed from the east side of the capital to reach the heights of being the first black player to captain England.

'I feel I have had much in common with Paul,' added Campbell.

It is all about the moment that changes the direction you are heading. Cheesewright says: 'There was a number of pitches that he played on. I saw him for school and his club teams. I followed him and nobody else even knew about him. But he was very stubborn, a very strong character. One team he played for wanted him as their centre-half but he wanted to be centre-forward and would not play in the other role.'

Cheesewright did not want to lose out on him. 'I kept ensuring I was a bloody nuisance because I wanted him at Spurs. I used to take him there myself and then he became very independent. Because he did not want me to show any special favours to him ahead of the other boys, he went on his own, even though it would take an hour and a half to reach Tottenham's training ground.

'We did not live too far away from each other and I offered to take Sol in my car because it meant him getting a tube to Liverpool Street and then a train to Tottenham,' says Cheesewright. 'But in the end he would not have any of it. It was him being proud and wanting to do things for himself.'

He stood out to Cheesewright because he was so tall in the schools' matches that he used to watch and after returning from Lilleshall, he had the chance to make a name for himself when he was selected for the England Under-18 side for the European Championships, a tournament that they won.

Back at Spurs, Campbell was playing up front in the youth team and Cheesewright remembers: 'He was awesome. He scored goals like nothing else on earth, he was frightening, he was that good. But I persuaded him to go centre-half because I thought his game would develop better in that role . . . all the staff were saying he was big, awkward and clumsy but Spurs had been struggling for a good centre-half for ten years and once he got in the role, they could see how good he was.'

Now the whole country knows about his talent, and FIFA has recognised it too. Campbell scored the opening goal of England's World Cup finals campaign in the draw with Sweden and his stature grew during the 2001–02 season.

There was stunned surprise at the Arsenal training ground in the summer of 2001 when they announced that a new player was about to be unveiled. Such had become Campbell's stock that he had been talking to clubs across Europe after taking advantage of the Bosman rule and leaving Spurs. Real Madrid looked the favourites, so when Campbell walked out from behind a screen at Arsenal there was genuine shock.

Sol has become one of a handful of players to make the switch across the capital's two arch enemies. He handled the Arsenal–Tottenham games with the confidence that now soars through the way he plays. Cheesewright was not surprised. 'He had never let things get to him so this would not either. It is part of his character that he has never lost. When he was 13 and I first knew him, he was so cool about situations that you wonder if anything would shake him – and I am not sure if it would. It was the way he developed . . . and he is one of the best defenders in the world.

'I had no fears when there was all the pressure building up towards the game about how Sol would be going back to Spurs. How would he be? He would be the usual Sol because he has this control in his mind that he can just shut off everything he does and make sure he concentrates without a problem on what he has to do. That is what makes him such a great player.'

But he was a rarity in one respect for a youngster that came from West Ham Park and played schools and club football on the local scene. Besides a brief appearance, he was not a member of the team that has become a production line for professional players . . .

## 12. The Legend of Senrab

IT WAS ON 5 APRIL 1952 THAT IVAN ARTHUR BROADIS, A MIDFIELD player with Manchester City, made his England debut against Scotland at Hampden Park in Glasgow. He progressed to represent his country on 14 more occasions after his first game brought a 2–1 victory, and he even featured at the 1954 World Cup finals in Switzerland.

While the Second World War was never likely to fade from memory, new heroes were being sought and at St Paul's Way School in the Bow area of east London, there was no bigger hero than this man who pulled on the white shirt of England during a career in which he also played for Newcastle. The rise of successful footballers in the east end cannot be attributed solely to the minimal international achievements of Broadis, but in the 1950s he was a superstar for the boys to cling on to in a country that was still rebuilding its way back to normality.

There were photographs of him in the school, his performances were analysed by the youngsters during break-time and there was no greater star pupil than this player.

Fifty years later, Fred Carter, an ex-pupil, is sitting in the upstairs workshop of his upholstery business in Roman Road in Stepney, remembering St Paul's and the way his friends and he used to look up to Broadis. Behind him on the wall is a photograph of a team of smiling boys with a trophy in front of them, taken after yet another triumph.

If Broadis was the first, he was anything but the last to emerge from this part of London. No other London team, perhaps no other English team, has developed so many youngsters who have progressed to the top flight than the club called Senrab. There is hardly anyone involved in Sunday League football in this area who has not heard of the team; they are the Manchester United, Liverpool and Arsenal of the east-end boys' scene all rolled into one.

Many of the brightest stars and rising stars of the Premiership started with Senrab: Ledley King (Spurs), John Terry (Chelsea), Lee Bowyer (Leeds), Muzzy Izzet (Leicester), Ashley Cole (Arsenal), for 45 minutes at least, J. Lloyd Samuels (Aston Villa), Paul Konchesky (Charlton), John Fortune (Charlton), Jermaine Defoe (West Ham), Darren Purse (Birmingham), Leon Knight (Chelsea), Bobby Zamora (Brighton) and Ade Akinbiyi (Leicester). Some of these stars played together in the same Senrab side, and they were nothing short of lethal.

Senrab celebrated their 40th anniversary in 2002. It is a good time to reflect on a team started by a gentleman named Billy Payne, who was keen to become involved in Sunday League football. He lived in Barnes Street in Tower Hamlets, and he was desperate for a catchy name; he looked at his road, switched the letters in Barnes around, and Senrab was formed.

One of the first big-name players to emerge from the team was Ray Wilkins in the late 1960s and early '70s. Even Glenn Roeder, the manager at West Ham, remembers Senrab as one of the teams everyone knew about on Hackney Marshes. The progression of Senrab players to enter the ranks of the professional game has never been greater than in the past decade.

Bowyer, who lived in Poplar as a boy and started his career at Charlton before his move to Leeds, and Izzet, who helped Turkey finish a mesmerising third at the 2002 World Cup finals, played in the same Senrab team. But they were two years above the roll call of players that now line up in the Premiership together, with one having made a record in the League that could last for a long time.

On Saturday, 9 December 2001, Spurs were away to Bradford at

Valley Parade. Ten seconds after the kick-off, Ledley King fired a shot from the edge of the box that took a deflection and gave goalkeeper Matt Clarke no chance: it was the quickest goal in Premiership history. King is 22. He has been described as the new Sol Campbell at Spurs: tall, lanky, a good defender, he is a player with big prospects. An east Londoner who was discovered not by a scout with an eye for a talent but by an assistant schoolteacher who was monitoring the children during a lunch break.

Fred Carter's son James played for Senrab at the time, and the boy's closest friend at Olga school was King. They lived near each other just off the Roman Road and were inseparable as children. 'My wife worked at the school and she used to say that James had a mate twice as big as him,' says Carter, who helped out at Senrab by driving the boys to games.

Carter recalls how his wife told him to take Ledley along to one of the games, after seeing the way he kicked the ball in the playground in a football game with their son. They were both six at the time and the next occasion that Senrab were training, Ledley joined his best friend.

'He was a natural from the start,' recalls Carter. 'Ledley as a footballer is where he was meant to be. I don't think he could have done another job, he could not have adapted to anything else.

'I would pick him up, or he would be staying at our house, and we would be leaving and he would forget his boots. But when he stepped out onto that football pitch, he was a totally different person. Assured, in control and you did not have to tell him anything.'

King is now a strapping centre-half with good control, a position he played in for the young Senrab side with the additional bonus of being their taker of corner kicks because he was so good. In one of his first games for Senrab, he scored direct from a corner in a cup final. 'It was unbelievable when you think of the way some seven year olds take corners,' says Carter.

King is growing in confidence with every game he plays for Spurs. Carter's own son played for Gillingham but a serious back injury forced him to quit the game, while King has progressed to represent England Under-21s. He is multi-talented, with an ability that Carter feels he can take some of the credit for: when Ledley used to play at James's house, Fred would take them over to the local park for extra training and he made them use their left foot whenever the ball came to them – and it worked.

King has stayed close to Carter, who did such a good job in those extra sessions that when George Graham was Tottenham's manager, he asked the mentor what he thought Ledley's natural foot was.

'I told him that it is his right, but most people think he is left-footed,' said Carter. 'That is how well he had made it work. It was just simply these training afternoons where we would knock the ball around with a few kids with this one stipulation. I am sure Ledley could take a corner or even a penalty with either foot and he does not have to worry about what side he is defending on.'

The list of names that have played for Senrab who have gone on to the big time is even longer than that of Ridgeway Rovers, the side that produced the game's leading player, David Beckham. There is a belief among many ex-members of the squad that they progressed to the Premiership level because of the way they all used to feed off of each other. The area brought them together, and the combination of their talents fine-tuned what might otherwise not have been developed.

Ironically, they all played in different positions. John Terry, now a centre-half, played in midfield, J. Lloyd Samuels, a left-back, played up front and when Senrab faced their fiercest rivals, Puma, Ashley Cole, now the England left-back, was a striker.

Every year Senrab would take part in a tournament in Southport during the school holidays. It was a week-long event, with teams from different age groups. One year when they arrived, King was walking past the swings in a play area when a kid came hurtling against him and broke his arm. He needed to have an operation but the team still performed in the tournament without him.

Before a game against the defending champions, from Lancashire, their team manager sought out the Senrab officials, including manager Paul Rolls and Carter, to let them know that his side had not been beaten for years in this event. When the match finished with Senrab victorious by 15–0, the opposition manager could not believe it. Carter says: 'I told him to keep the programme because one day he could reflect on the players he had been watching that day.' Where is that valuable programme now?

Carter calls himself King's minder. He is not there for protection, but in case the Spurs star ever needs any advice.

King's arrival at Spurs came by chance. Along with James Carter, he was training at Orient, who had spotted them first. Tottenham's youth development officer, John Moncur, told Fred Carter he wanted to see James. 'I told him I would bring James and the best centre-half in England,' recalls Fred.

Spurs, who were managed at the time by Gerry Francis, agreed to give King his first professional contract at the age of 16. They offered him a four-year deal but Carter stalled on letting him sign it. By then he had got to know the football agent Jonathan Barnett and contacted him for advice. Barnett had never heard of King, who was an England schoolboy, but Carter says: 'He told me to ring back in five minutes. I did and he said he had rung around a few clubs and was Ledley sure that he wanted to go to Spurs. I told him he was but he advised me that they sign for only two years because when he was 18, he would not want two more years of wages based on when he was 16.'

King played in the Worthington Cup final against Blackburn in 2001. Spurs lost 2–1 at the Millennium Stadium in Cardiff, where he was blamed for the winning goal as his error allowed Andy Cole to score.

'Ledley has always liked to play football,' said Carter. 'What they are trying to teach him at Spurs is that every now and then they want him to hump the ball away.'

King has remained close friends with the Carters, regularly popping in to see Fred and often reminiscing about the times they shared at Senrab, and in particular how so many players have progressed in different positions from where they started out.

Of the other Senrab players, Terry has had to contend with a number of high-profile off-the-field problems at Chelsea, but in a team that is jam-packed with more foreign players than any other in the Premiership, he has been able to secure his place in the side. Izzet's brother Kermal, another ex-Senrab player, is now with Colchester and looks set to follow his sibling's success. Brighton, who were promoted to the First Division in season 2001–02, have Zamora in their side. Zamora joined the same Senrab side as King and Terry and there is hardly a brighter striking prospect outside of the Premiership. His goals helped the south-coast side to promotion and he has been linked with moves in the region of £5 million.

All of these players are east London boys who came through a local club system to make a career out of what used to be nothing more than a regular meeting of friends on a Sunday. Zamora could end up becoming the best of them if the progress he has made carries on in the same style over the next few seasons.

In summer 2002 there may have been a glimpse of the future for the senior squad when the Under-21s competed in the European Championships in Switzerland. In the first game in Zurich, they beat the hosts 2–1 with Defoe scoring after just two minutes. Zamora appeared as a substitute in their other two games, replacing his former Senrab team mate in the final one, against Portugal.

When Zamora was first picked for the Under-21 squad in May 2002, having scored 34 goals in the previous season and 32 out of 46 league games in 2001–02, when Brighton won the title, international manager David Platt said: 'His record over the last two seasons speaks for itself and I'm looking forward to working with him in training. He has a natural talent for scoring goals and that is priceless.'

The Premiership beckons; he will surely follow the example of Konchesky, who plays for Charlton in the same side as John Fortune, another graduate of this school of east London excellence. They are both now regulars in the side.

'It was an amazing team at Senrab and we won so many matches,' says Konchesky. 'And then it is equally amazing how two of us have ended here. We talk about those days with some great memories.

'It is strange, though, the way things go. When you are young you play in teams with the hope that one day one of you might make it. You hope it will be you but then when you see so many of them progressing from Senrab, it is hard to believe. It is an area where a lot of talent comes from, and they have had and still do have a great reputation.'

Konchesky and Fortune have become members of a solid squad at The Valley under manager Alan Curbishley, while Terry is being talked of as a future England player, if he can avoid some of the headlines that followed him last season. Fortune was a centre-forward with Senrab, but as his career moved on, so did his position – he is now a centre-half.

But no one has progressed better than Cole, an Arsenal fan as a youngster, who has filled the vacant England role on the left side of their defence, and can attack if needed (he is such an effective wing-back) with ease. This is no surprise to those who grew up with him, because Cole was a prolific striker for a team called Puma, Senrab's rivals. When Arsenal meet Spurs now, in either the FA Cup or the League, it is like being back on Hackney Marshes or Wanstead Flats, another east London setting.

Cole used to play regularly against King and the first time they met, the future Gunner triumphed as Puma won 3–1; Senrab never lost to them again.

'We were just east end lads coming together and making a good team,' said King in an interview in the *Daily Telegraph*. 'I played with John Terry at Senrab. He was in midfield and I was centre-half. Last season in the England Under-21s, I was in midfield and John was at the back. Ashley was a centre-forward back on Wanstead Flats. It's funny to see the way our positions have changed.

'The pitches at Wanstead Flats weren't the best, but that wasn't important to us. We just wanted to play. I have always been single-minded, always wanted to be a footballer. Growing up in London, there could have been distractions but my friends never got themselves into trouble, which helped me.'

On one occasion, when he was eight, Cole played for Senrab, as did Sol Campbell for a time before moving to Rippleway Newham. Cole was brought across for a game, starting as a substitute and then coming on for the second half. But he did not return for future games because Puma were his side. He wanted to play full matches and was a prolific scorer who operated along the left flank.

Scouts used to watch Puma and Senrab, and they homed in on the range of talent of boys from the vicinity when they were all selected to play in the same London Boys' team.

Often King and Cole would play together for a representative side from Islington and Camden schools, which in 1996 won the London Corinthian Trophy by beating Tower Hamlets 4–2 . . . at Highbury of all places. By then Cole was on the verge of becoming an Arsenal apprentice and fulfilling his dream of playing for the club he supported.

Cole was born in Stepney, in the heart of the east end, on 20 December 1980. He has become an established part of the international scene after his impressive emergence in the Arsenal side. He was selected for the first international side that Sven-Goran Eriksson named and made his debut in March 2001, away to Albania. The manager was quick to praise the way he reacted after being hit on the head by a coin thrown from the hostile crowd. Now he is a regular, and you suspect his name is one of the first on the manager's list when he selects his team.

But the significance of his success is sometimes lost: at the time of writing, Cole is only 22. This point is often forgotten because of the maturity he shows in his game.

During the World Cup finals in Japan, the occasions when Wayne Bridge of Southampton came into the team as left-back allowed Cole the opportunity to move ahead, and he looked just as at home there as he did in the defensive role.

Wilkins, an old Senrab player who progressed to play for England

and had extremely successful spells at both Chelsea, where he made his name, and Manchester United, was one of the first stars to emerge from this team.

But the Senrab story is far from over. Knight, at Chelsea, is being described as one of the best young talents in the game, developed by Senrab while Defoe at West Ham has fast been making a name for himself during the European Championships in the summer and with the aim of pressing for a regular place in the first-team squad.

Often when a prediction is made for the England team for the 2006 World Cup finals, Defoe is in it; that is the level of progression for a player who has been on loan at Bournemouth, where he scored at almost a record rate.

Some players are born to be superstars: their fate takes them on a course that so many want to share. Some respond to the success of their friends, like the boys from Senrab did. Playing with the best can bring the best out of you and Senrab, who celebrated 40 years of their existence in February, have set a standard that has taken their former boys to the levels of the game they used to dream of on those Sunday games in east London.

From Senrab to England; Wilkins did it and he set a trend . . .

## 13. Time to be Frank

ON ONLY THREE OCCASIONS HAVE A FATHER AND SON represented England. It happened first in 1963, when George Eastham Jnr played against Brazil at Wembley, 28 years after his dad had made his only appearance for the country in a match away to Holland. It was 26 years until it happened again, when Bobby Robson, the England manager, selected Nigel Clough to play against Chile, repeating the feat of his father Brian, whose two internationals came in 1960. Frank Lampard Snr played for England twice, once in 1972 under Sir Alf Ramsey, in a 1–1 draw at Wembley with Yugoslavia. Not until eight years later did he win his second cap, when Ron Greenwood, his former manager at West Ham and now in charge of the national side, called him into the team for a centenary match against Australia in Sydney.

On Sunday, 10 October 1999, the east end of London had enormous reason to be proud when Frank Lampard Jnr, now of Chelsea, then with West Ham, made his England debut in a friendly against Belgium at Sunderland's Stadium of Light in a 2–1 victory, 19 years after his father, Frank Snr, had represented the country.

The young Lampard's game has since taken him to a multi-million move across London, from east to west, and a lifestyle a long way away from when his father first started out in the game. But he still has many friends from the east end and the area will never be forgotten by him or his father, whose upbringing and career encompasses the majority of the elements that have taken us on this journey from Bobby Moore, through the decades to the arrival of

David Beckham and beyond into a future where the area will surely develop more stars.

Frank Snr was born in East Ham but when he was only two, his father was killed in a car accident and he and his mother went to live with his grandparents in West Ham, in Liverpool Road, of all places, just a few miles from Upton Park. Was he destined to become a footballer? Well, maybe fate does play its part, but when Lampard was born in 1948 there was not a great deal of choice for a youngster who came from an area that, while it was not exactly deprived, was hardly one of the most thriving communities in the capital.

Lampard lived in Canning Town and today, whatever time, night or day, you travel through there the roads are always busy; the growing Asian community has changed the structure of the area, with many shops open all night. Today many fans of West Ham still live as close to the ground as the man who progressed to spend 18 years at the club did. 'Everyone is still as crazy about West Ham as I was,' he says.

He played 665 times for West Ham after making his debut in 1967; it was almost *Boy's Own* stuff. He joined the club as an apprentice in 1964 when they were on the verge of being the most talked-about team in England. They won the FA Cup that year and the European Cup-Winners' Cup 12 months later and then Moore led England to World Cup glory.

'I was 15 when I signed for West Ham and the early memories were great,' says Lampard. 'Everyone trained on the same ground. On one pitch you had Bobby Moore and you were on the other pitch and you could glance across to see him.'

But within a matter of years, Lampard did not have to look too far to see Moore because he was playing across the same back four and on away trips, he was in the next bed. Lampard and Moore were roommates for eight years at West Ham after the left-back had progressed into the first team.

'I learnt a lot from Bobby,' says Lampard. 'Off the field, he was the tidiest person in the world. He was always very organised; when he took his socks off at night, he would fold them up whereas everyone else would normally just throw them in the corner.

'It all started when I was a young boy and had just got into the side. For our away games up north, we used to go by train. It might have been my first or second away match in the team.

'We were travelling back and Bobby was sitting at the other end of the carriage with three other people. He pointed his finger towards me and told me to come and sit with them. That was it. Bobby made you so welcome.'

Lampard recalls how daunting it was to play alongside Moore at first. 'If you gave away a bad ball, he did not shout at you or swear at you, he just looked at you and that was enough,' he says.

But it was simply the fact he was 'Bobby Moore' that made him such an inspiration to Lampard.

'His whole mannerism was something to see when he played,' he says. 'He led by example; he was immaculate in his approach to the game and the way he conducted himself on the field.

'Some people were in awe of him because of who he was, and then once you got to know him, he was just a nice person. He always wanted to help you out, he liked company, he was not shy but a little bit inward until you brought him out.'

Lampard helped West Ham win the 1975 FA Cup, when they beat Fulham, a side that by then included Moore himself. Five years later, he enjoyed one of his finest moments, this time in an FA Cup semi-final replay against Everton at Elland Road. Lampard scored a dramatic winner, a goal that sent BBC commentator Barry Davies's voice spiralling skywards when the defender ran away to celebrate by running around the corner flag. The Hammers went on to beat Arsenal 1–0 in the final, with a goal by Trevor Brooking.

He had achieved his childhood ambition, like so many of his contemporaries, and those before and after him; the east end gave him the drive to succeed at sport and he was not going to allow anything to stand in the way of making it to the highest level that he could reach in the game.

'Football was always my ambition,' says Lampard. 'In those days, if you were not a footballer at 15, you went to work in the docks, or you became involved in petty crime. I knew what direction I wanted to take in life.

'Canning Town was a hard area. There were a lot of tough nuts around and though I don't want to sound too offish, it was a bit deprived. And that probably led to a fear that if you did not do something, then you might end up working in the docks in Royal Docks in Silvertown.

'With the petty crime that was around, you had an incentive to get out of that and to become a player was something that seemed achievable.'

Football or the docks? It was a similar choice to that which befell Harry Redknapp. Like Lampard he chose soccer and West Ham, and not only was Lampard his No. 2 at Upton Park, he is also his brother-in-law.

Lampard attended Pretoria Secondary Modern School in Canning Town from the age of 11 and an example of how football can lift children from the east end, especially those who are determined to succeed, came when a fellow pupil, the late John Charles, who was four years his senior, went on to join West Ham.

'When he went to a pro club it was like the highlight of what was happening in the area,' said Lampard. 'And as he had gone to the same school I used to look up to him and think to myself that it is possible to achieve the things that you want to.'

Back in the late 1950s, the area was divided into two schoolboy teams. Unlike now, when there is one side, Newham, then it was either East Ham or West Ham boys. Lampard played for the latter.

'In those days at our school we used to play on cinder pitches,' says Lampard. 'It really did help with your technique because you had to be a bit lively to keep the ball under control.

'When I left school at 15, grass was just starting to be laid at some of the schools and up until then you had only played on that when you were in the district team. In our area, they were all cinder pitches until the mid-1960s.

'But the pitches were not the key; just seeing people progress from where we were to pro clubs, guys like John Charles, made it the ambition of every kid that used to play to do somethng like that.'

Lampard was in the same West Ham boys team as Roger Cross, now an assistant to Glenn Roeder at West Ham, and he was another who has played on Hackney Marshes.

'From time to time an uncle used to be in goal for a team called Vikings,' says Lampard. 'They were a good amateur side at the Marshes. I used to go to watch him and I ended up playing in one of the games.'

By then the cattle grids had been replaced by a row of basins for players to wash themselves in after the matches – there were still no showers – and Lampard agrees that this no-nonsense approach was important. 'It toughens you up,' he says. 'You just had to get on with it.'

He had a fine career, with only Billy Bonds appearing in more matches for West Ham (793 to his 665) and when his days as a player came to an end at Upton Park, he was reacquainted with Moore. By 1985 Moore was in his second year as manager of Southend and he brought Lampard in as player-coach; the combination from over a decade earlier had been reunited.

Within nine months, though, Moore had left the club and Lampard followed him, but he returned to his roots at West Ham as assistant to Redknapp in 1994. The pair left in 2001 to be replaced by Glenn Roeder at an Upton Park ground that is changing too; the old main stand has been knocked down for a plush new building and while tradition cannot be ignored, the modern age means improvements are needed. And sometimes, when the past and the future collide, they can lead to some unexpected experiences.

Noel Cantwell, who had played such an important part in bringing Moore into the team, had a magical day back at the club for a reunion early in 2002 when they arranged for him and the rest of the former players who had been at the Upton Park celebration to stay over, instead of having to drive back when the party was finished. But they did not book them into a hotel. There are beds on site, and Cantwell could not believe what happened. Talk about a room with a view; Cantwell could not have asked for a better balcony scene when he woke up in the morning to the famous pitch where he had enjoyed so many good years and countless memories. The boxes in the Doc Martin Stand that are normally used for sponsors and guests to watch games can be turned into bedrooms, and it was there that Cantwell spent the night.

'It was amazing,' he said. 'The changing face of football eh? They quickly turn the rooms around, they are made into bedrooms and you can look out onto the pitch.'

It gave him a chance to reminisce about the years of helping to bring through some of the great stars of the game in the east end. He chuckles when he thinks of the money now involved in football and the profile that has taken it to a new level. With all the progress, the production line in this part of England is still maintaining a standard that was set during his days at the club. 'I love talking about the old times because there were so many great stories,' he says.

That was the start of the academy that brought on the Lampards and took them into the England record books, a route that was followed by another Hammer, Paul Ince, who was born in Bobby Moore country, nearby in Barking.

When Ince took the armband on 9 June 1993, chosen by manager Graham Taylor, it was the first time a black player had been made captain of the country. Ince was a hard-working midfielder who was inspirational in the Hammers' finest league season, 1986–87, when they finished third in the old First Division. They were serious contenders for a title won, inevitably in those days, by Liverpool.

He was also inspirational on the famous night in Rome 11 years later when England qualified for the 1998 World Cup. Ince suffered a gash on his head during the game but insisted he would carry on playing and did so, his shirt more red than white. Arguably, he has never played better for his country than that night.

Although he entered the record books as captain, his personal success concided with one of England's most humiliating defeats of modern times. The Foxboro Stadium in Massachusetts was the venue during the US Cup and England suffered the ignominy of losing 2–0 to America, 43 years after their only other defeat by them in the World Cup finals in Brazil.

Honour and embarrassment came at the same time for Ince, but the lead had been set and since then Sol Campbell has followed, to become another black captain of England.

As a youngster, Ince was one of the main players of his district side in Redbridge, attracting attention with the same never-say-die attitude that he is known for today. Snapped up by the then West Ham manager John Lyall, Ince progressed through their Youth Training Scheme to the first team and to the top of the game.

Long before, Lampard had taken Ince for a training session at Upton Park when he first arrived on the scene as a schoolboy, and he remembers it well. At the time, Greenwood was manager of West Ham and he had decreed that members of the playing staff should begin coaching. It was the usual path for a footballer, long before the days when they had alternative directions to take after their playing careers were finished, such as the now endless media outlets or the growing world of promotions.

Lampard says: 'I used to go to coach twice a week at night time at West Ham. One day I had these kids in the gym, and I used to take the Under-11s. I called them together to chat to them; they all came and as I started talking, this little kid just wandered off and starting kicking the ball against the wall.

'I called him back and said, "Don't do that again." I started talking again and he began to kick the ball as we were standing, while the others were listening.

'His name was Paul Ince; he was one of those kids who just wanted to play around with the ball all the time. He was a jolly lad and he stood out because of his ability.'

Ince progressed to the highest level, and by the time England reached the World Cup finals in France in 1998, where he had so bravely battled to help take them, he had the misfortune of being one of the penalty takers that missed in the shoot-out against Argentina that saw the country crash out of the competition.

Ince has had a fine career. After representing England at youth level he was at West Ham for five seasons before moving to Manchester United, sparking the anger of the West Ham fans by famously posing for a photograph in the red shirt before he had left Upton Park. Whenever he returns, they show they have not forgotten. He spent two years at Inter Milan in Italy, moving from Manchester United to one of the biggest club teams on the continent. Ultimately it did not work out as well as he had hoped – English players have traditionally failed to shine on the European club scene – and he returned for spells at Liverpool and Middlesbrough, which he left this summer to seek another stop-off point in his career at Wolverhampton Wanderers.

In his international career he played for England during the disappointing Euro 2000 Championships and the last of his appearances came in the final match of England's campaign in Belgium when they lost 3–2 to Romania. Ince had won 53 caps for England during an international career that had stretched nine years, and secured his place in the record books after being given the captaincy, albeit for one of the gloomiest days in England's football history.

Frank Lampard's son had made the England team in 1999, on a changing tide that now sees Ince no longer on the scene. A wave of youngsters have entered the international picture in a squad which has a different structure under a new manager, a man who arrived from Italy via Sweden. As England manager, Sven-Goran Eriksson surveyed the weekend fixtures in the Premiership once he was in the country, and he chose to watch his first game in the east end of London.

By October 2000, the national game had reached one of its lowest ebbs, during a time of changing faces and decision-making at the Football Association (and changing premises for that matter, when they moved from the long-term home in Lancaster Gate to Soho). One event had sparked the need for change.

Grand old Wembley Stadium was fast becoming outdated in a world where the modern arena is not complete without some sort of moveable seating or retractable roof. A long-running row meant refurbishment would not take place until after the first match of the qualifying campaign for the 2002 World Cup finals.

It was fitting that the last game at Wembley should be against Germany, the opponents in the final 34 years earlier, when England won the World Cup. But what a difference between then and now. Then it was all about triumph and glory; now a goal by Dietmar Hamann from a long-range free kick subjected England to a 1–0 defeat and less than an hour after the game, Kevin Keegan resigned as manager.

The atmosphere at Wembley that afternoon was a lifetime away from how it had been on that day in 1966; a solemn crowd was left wondering why the national game, on the back of that disastrous campaign at the European Championships in the previous summer, had suffered so much. How ironic that there should be such a shift in direction. The country had been on a high that week because the Olympic Games in Sydney had just finished and with 11 gold medals, Britain was celebrating its greatest haul for 80 years and probably their best team performance ever in terms of the number of countries competing.

Football brought those high spirits back down to earth again, and the lasting memory for many who left the game that day would be of a cold, worn-out Wembley, a defeat, and the possibility that the country might not make the World Cup finals. The stadium that had made Moore an international icon and Geoff Hurst a record-breaker was hardly paying any respect to the memories of yesteryear. It was time for change, dramatic change.

Many people see that day as a turning point, not quite as dramatic as in 1966 when England won the World Cup, but a significant step forward to a period when, perhaps, the country would be in the position to be serious challengers again for the greatest prize in the game.

Fast-forward 14 weeks to Saturday, 13 January 2001, the second weekend of a new year. A crowd of 26,014 have their eyes trained on just one place at West Ham's Upton Park ground, high up in the main stand where the directors sit. An unfamiliar, bespectacled man slips into his seat and waves to acknowledge the crowd's acclaim. It is probably just coincidence that Eriksson had chosen to go to the east end to make his debut on a tour of endless games, but here he was. Eriksson, a Swede, the first foreigner to manage England, had come to the rescue of the country; it is a sign of a changing era and a bridge between the past and the present as new players move into West Ham to build on a tradition that Moore, Hurst and Peters created.

Eriksson had heard about Joe Cole, the new young star from the academy, and he wanted to see for himself what all the fuss was about. Cole started in the game on the day of Sven's visit, and although the Hammers lost 2–0, Eriksson had seen enough. He brought the youngster in to his senior squad for the World Cup finals, when the manager turned England's stuttering progress around and took them to Japan, though they were knocked out in the quarter-finals by Brazil.

Eriksson has been to Upton Park as often as any of the grounds during his enormous amount of travelling across Britain in search of players. Cole did not start a game in Japan, but Eriksson was impressed from the moment he saw him.

'Joe Cole is a big talent and can do things which most other players can't,' said Eriksson after the player had made his debut in the 4–0 defeat of Mexico at Derby's Pride Park ground. 'He has a special talent with dribbling and I have always liked him.'

Everything, it seems, goes back to 1966. In 2002, there was hope that the omens would be with England again, because three players from West Ham – just as 36 years earlier – had been included in the World Cup final squad.

But while Trevor Sinclair played, David James and Cole did not and England could not match the boys of that summer of triumph.

Under the new management of Roeder, West Ham will aim to carry on producing the type of players that have flowed through their ranks and into the England squad. In Moore's day, the youth system at the club was flourishing and the same is true today, with West Ham having so many links to the teams from local schools and clubs in the area.

As time moves on, West Ham attempt to keep to their tradition of playing attractive football, and Cole is set to become the latest to join the list of east end stars with the praise he receives and his ability to show such fantastic trickery and skill on the ball; he excites a crowd when he is in possession, which cannot be said of too many English players in the game today.

The east end club has had so many players that have been great entertainers: Brooking and Alan Devonshire were among the best in the 1970s and '80s at West Ham, while a matter of miles away at Leyton Orient, another landmark for the area arrived on 22 December 1996.

Peter Shilton had been one of the finest goalkeepers in England's history, winning a record 125 caps and in a career that had begun 30 years earlier, he was now on the verge of another groundbreaking success. At the age of 47, and still looking fit, trim and with outstanding agility, he had joined Third Division Leyton Orient and when they played Brighton three days before Christmas he celebrated his 1,000th domestic appearance.

Typically, he kept a clean sheet as Orient won 2–0, and the match became a great occasion for the club, as it was shown live on television and Shilton walked out onto the pitch to a fanfare to commemorate his achievement. His career ended five games later, when he retired.

It is a feat that might not be repeated. But in a time where the game has changed in England with a fresh approach to how the national team is run following the arrival of Eriksson, will the stars of tomorrow have a place to display their skills to a country in a national stadium? The long-running saga of Wembley has become an endless argument of ifs, buts, maybes and there is still no solution to rebuilding a venue that remains the most famous football ground in the world.

The nine World Cups that have passed since 1966 might have produced as much drama as that of 36 years ago, but Wembley still remains the place that more footballers want to play at than anywhere else. The greatest irony could lie in Hackney Marshes, and the future plans that are being talked about for that area. The British Olympic Association (BOA) have earmarked the land either side of the Marshes as one of their venues for a site to stage The Games, should the country bid for them.

It would mean a revamp for the Marshes, because a new stadium could find itself being built on the area where the many football pitches lie now. If it is constructed on the other side of the road, that land might be redeveloped completely into a modern-day Olympic park.

As yet these are only plans, but in 1999 proposals were drawn up to use the area around the Marshes for a site for a stadium to stage the World Athletics Championships, an idea that was rejected. Since then the BOA have been linked with the Marshes as one of the areas they would consider redeveloping, should an Olympic bid become a feasible option. Many believe that this land is a prime site on which to construct a new sporting home. There have been continual problems with parking and access to Wembley, but the Marshes area is wide enough to have sufficient room on which to build the venues needed to stage a Games.

But where would this leave Wembley? And would the 'Mecca' of the Marshes be destroyed for good? It seems unlikely – tradition might not allow it to be wiped away. Since October 2000, when Wembley stadium closed its doors to competitive football for the last time, the rows have grown and costs have increased; it costs a fortune for the stadium to lie unused and untouched. It is estimated that £100 million of tax-payers' money has been spent on Wembley since 2000 – and that has been just to keep it as it stands now.

The success of Eriksson's men travelling around the country to play their games, from Villa Park to Anfield to Old Trafford, has left the FA in a delicate position over the need to have a national stadium in London. It is an argument that is finely balanced; if it is a national team, then it should have a home all to itself but, alternatively, should there not be an option for players to be seen in action by people in different parts of England?

The process of change cannot be avoided, but Wembley seems to have been left behind. Even leading up to that final match against Germany over two years ago, Wembley had been run down to a state where it was no longer anywhere near the best ground in the country. It had stood still while club sides moved with the times and there is growing unrest in football over why this problem could not have been addressed as part of long-term improvements, rather than a date being set for rebuilding to start but that never happening because the funds were not in place and different bodies were not in agreement over how it should look.

I remember the thrill of going on the Wembley tour; it was a chance to visit the stadium, walk out of the tunnel and go up the same stairs that Moore had climbed to lift the World Cup. No longer.

In the build-up to this summer's World Cup, the television channels were packed with nostalgic re-runs of the past finals. They showed the whole match from 1966 when England beat West Germany, but still the problem rolls on about what to do with the stadium. And each month that the Wembley saga continues without any new development, so the arena of the landmark match of 1966 becomes a less significant place. The memory of the achievement of Moore and Co. deserves more respect than that.

## 14. Home Comforts

THERE IS SOMETHING CHARMING ABOUT SUPPORTING A TEAM
from a lower division, or so I have always found among friends who
have chosen to show their allegiances away from a side that do not
play in Europe every season, or always reach the FA Cup semi-final,
or have to play on Sundays because television channels want to screen
their big games.

The team you support is one of the biggest decisions you can make
and you cannot change your mind. Once those colours are hoisted in
the air, they cannot be lowered or transferred – it is just not right.

Choosing a lower-division team allows you not to raise your
expectations too high: if we achieve promotion this season it is a
bonus, but if we stay up and avoid relegation it is a success.

Supporting and then reporting on your dream team makes for some
great moments: getting paid to watch football was good enough on a
Saturday, but being paid to watch the football team you want to watch
anyway is a busman's holiday . . . in Barbados.

Two stories stand out for me about my affiliation with a team that
always makes you feel part of them. When I started supporting
Leyton Orient, I became sick of the jokes about the match starting
once we got there because of the lack of supporters, but one Saturday
afternoon the joke became a reality.

My father and I liked our regular seats so much – good view, near
the exit, front row, all the usual stuff – that we booked them through
the ticket office on a match-by-match basis. On some occasions we
missed games, so it was easier to do it that way rather than by buying

season tickets. At some time or another we had filled out a questionnaire at Orient, with our telephone number on it, and handed it back into the ticket office. This led to an extraordinary afternoon.

That day we were running late and had not left for the game against Brighton, even though it was just gone half past two. As we were on our way out of our house in Essex, about a 15-minute drive from Brisbane Road, the telephone rang. 'Hello, Mr Lewis, it is Sue from the Orient ticket office,' said the voice. 'We are just checking that you are coming to the game today.' They were not quite waiting for us for the match to start, but it was close: Orient were ringing us up to see if we were on our way.

On a Saturday afternoon in January 1989 I realised again that local teams can provide moments in your life that you could not make up.

My photograph appeared regularly in the local newspaper that I worked for alongside my by-line when I was reporting football from Leyton Orient, and my voice would beam out across the capital as I covered the match for London radio station LBC.

A week before this particular Saturday game, I had got engaged and my future father-in-law was an Orient supporter, with a season ticket for a seat just in front of the press box. During the half-time announcements, suddenly there was a pause before the man on the public address system spoke again: he would like to congratulate Richard Lewis of the *Walthamstow Guardian* and LBC on his recent engagement, a little bit of information slipped his way from the man occupying the seat in row Z of Brisbane Road's main stand. Luckily no one can see you turn red with embarrassment when you have a pair of headphones on and a microphone to your face.

Ninety minutes after the game, I was walking to my car, lugging my heavy radio equipment, when I noticed three of the toughest-looking men I have ever seen walking towards me. It was getting dark, what crowd there was had long gone and I quickly threw the radio gear into the car, because one against three man-mountains just does not go.

I was not quick enough; they were there by the car.

'Excuse me mate,' shouted one of them.

'Yes,' I replied, quaking.

'We just want to say . . . congratulations on your engagement.'

On they walked, leaving me to drive home in total disbelief.

In my first season as an Orient fan the team beat Norwich, Blackburn, Chelsea and Middlesbrough to reach the semi-finals of the FA Cup against Arsenal at Chelsea's Stamford Bridge. I could not sleep the night before the match; it was my first year as a fan and their greatest year, the furthest this club had ever progressed in the competition.

Within minutes of the start of the game, Orient looked good but by half-time they were trailing 2–0 to goals from Malcolm McDonald and we lost 3–0.

When Orient reached the Third Division play-off final at Wembley in 1998, I was allowed by my employers on the *Daily Express* to miss covering another sporting event that day to report on my team at the Venue of Legends.

I had missed out in 1978, when I was convinced we would be in the FA Cup final, but playing Scunthorpe, in front of a half-full Wembley, would be acceptable enough. Orient lost the game 1–0, but it did not matter: I had given up hope long ago that they would provide me with some true cherished moments.

When Orient had previously reached the old Fourth Division play-off final in 1989, when it used to be a two-legged competition, they met Wrexham. The goals of Alan Comfort had been one of the keys to their progress but Orient had not been guaranteed a play-off place and he had arranged to get married on the Saturday of the second leg of the final.

But Orient could not afford to be without their star man. They won the game 2–1 to celebrate promotion, and within minutes of the end of the game, as the champagne flowed among the players, Comfort was whisked away by helicopter for the next part of his big afternoon.

Covering a local team can be great fun, because everyone is happy to talk to you, there is no media queue for the weekly press conference with the manager (who, in those days, was Frank Clark, the former Newcastle and Nottingham Forest full-back) but always I had to remember not to be too biased. Once on the radio I said 'we' were leading, but it was never picked up by the editor in the studio. Perhaps he was an Orient fan too.

Travelling to away games would always bring some great stories, because the club would genuinely be pleased to see that you had made the effort to come and report on them; never more so than on a grim day in Scarborough when the match had ended 0–0. There was controversy during the game with a number of awful tackles, and the bad feeling spilt over afterwards when Orient's players were not allowed to use the club bar. They quickly boarded their coach to leave as soon as they could.

I had decided to spend the weekend in Scarborough with my fiancée and she had come to the game with me, sitting in front of the press box. I have never agreed with reporters bringing their wives into the press area, however, and will never forget one day at Leyton Orient, in the middle of a post-match conference with Frank Clark after the game, when the door of the press room opened behind him. In walked the reporter covering the travelling team, followed by his wife, without apologising, and he stood there taking notes. Clark looked at him, bemused.

Back to Scarborough. Furious Clark had chosen to give his comments to myself and a reporter from our rival paper, who had also travelled up to see the game, while we were standing by the team coach. He was seething and nothing could calm the anger on his face.

My fiancée was standing apart from us waiting. Suddenly she burst into uncontrollable laughter. Four players on the team coach had stripped naked, just for her, and at this point Clark turned around, exploded into hilarity himself and the press conference began to flow as normal. Can you imagine that happening if I was the local reporter covering Arsenal? I would not even be allowed near the coach.

Sure, it is all about priorities and Arsène Wenger would not have only two reporters waiting to talk to him after a game, but there is something spectacularly rewarding about being able to pass judgement on the team that you support. Most fans can spend the game shouting and screaming but getting nowhere; I could stay quiet for 90 minutes and still know that what I really wanted to say would actually be heard.

Not, of course, that I ever let on in the columns of the *Walthamstow Guardian* that I was an Orient fan.

In the season that Orient reached the FA Cup semi-final, the star of the side was Peter Kitchen, who scored some phenomenal goals, none better than the two he put home at Chelsea in the fifth-round replay. He was my Orient hero, a fact I did not reveal when I used to interview him regularly after he returned to the club during my time as a reporter there.

Money has always been tight at the club. On occasions in the early 1970s, they had to pass a bucket around among the crowd to help bolster funds. Former manager George Petchey remembers the time the roof on the dressing-room caved in not long after he took over.

'I was told there was no way that it could be repaired because there were no funds to do so,' he says. In the end he persuaded a local building company to do it for nothing.

The arrival of Barry Hearn, an accountant by trade, was a vital acquisition in 1996 because he ensured financial stability, and now, at a time when many lower-division clubs are in real danger because of the loss of the ITV Digital funding, the Orient chairman has ensured the books are balancing without the need to call for help from the administrators.

It is amazing to think that back in the 1950s and '60s, the non-League scene in the east of London would attract crowds that not even Premiership clubs can bring in today. Walthamstow Avenue were one of the great sides of that period. They won the Amateur Cup at Wembley in 1952 in front of 100,000 people when they beat Leyton 2–1, and nine years later, regained the trophy by defeating West Auckland by the same scoreline. It is hard to believe that Wembley would be full to watch two amateur sides play, but it was.

The changing face of the modern game and the financial pressures that go with it saw the side merge in 1990 with close rivals Leytonstone-Ilford. They played under the joint name of Redbridge

Forest, a team that has now become Dagenham and Redbridge, a side that reached the third round of the FA Cup in 2001 and 2002 and just missed out on promotion into the Football League.

Time moves on and the tradition of the game has to change, but today the gulf has never been wider between amateur and professional sides. The amateur cup dissolved in 1974; it was replaced in sort by the FA Vase but most teams set their targets at the FA Trophy title.

The non-League stage always had the ability to bring through players that made it in the professional games: I remember watching Warren Barton storm down the wing for Leytonstone-Ilford before he left for a fine career with Maidstone, Wimbledon, Newcastle and now Derby. Nowadays, any youngster who shows some talent is normally signed up by clubs before they have left junior school, so today it is rare for players to move from non-League to the top level. There are exceptions to the rule, such as Barry Hayles, who has progressed from Stevenage Borough into the Premiership with Fulham.

Yet without the fabric of sides such as Orient, the game would be lost to the real fan, the one who does not set his or her standards too high because it will only bring disappointment and when success is in the air, it takes you to such a high that it is worth the wait until the next time it comes around.

From the back of the main stand at Orient's Brisbane Road ground, you can see across the whole of the east end: a wide stretch of roads with little grassland. But in the immediate vicinity is the area that provides the link: Hackney Marshes. I once saw the Marshes while travelling across the capital in a tiny plane and it looked so small; the goal posts were hardly visible and I wondered what it would be like to have this view on a Sunday morning.

I would not know where to look first, I suspect; for a goal on pitch 21, a fight on pitch 47 or the emergence of the east end's latest star on pitch 84, looking to follow in the footsteps of so many before him.

The breeding ground remains alive and kicking.

# Appendix: Biographies of the Players

## ALLEN, DENNIS AND LES
*Les: Born: 4.9.37, Dagenham*
*Dennis: Born: 2.3.39, Dagenham*
Les Allen was an amateur at Tottenham before joining Chelsea by way of Briggs Sports. He played 44 times for Chelsea before moving to Spurs in exchange for Johnny Brooks in 1959. In the Double season of 1960–61 Allen scored 23 league goals and four in the FA Cup, but the arrival of Jimmy Greaves left him struggling for first-team football. He moved to QPR in 1965, winning the League Cup in 1967. His son Clive scored 49 goals for Spurs in 1986–87. Brother Dennis started at Charlton before moving to Reading, where he clocked up over 400 appearances before finishing his career at Bournemouth.

## BECKHAM, DAVID
*Born: 2.5.75, Leytonstone*
The best-known footballer, worldwide, of his generation. He has grown into a player of outstanding maturity and skill. He was appointed England captain in late 2000, just over two years after being sent off in the World Cup finals in France for kicking Argentinian Diego Simeone. As a child he played for the junior team Ridgeway Rovers, and in 1986 he won the final of the Bobby Charlton Soccer Skills competition to get noticed. United kept track of him and on his 14th birthday they signed him on schoolboy terms. Despite a brief period on loan at Preston, he has never looked back. He caught the

public's attention with a spectacular goal from inside his own half against Wimbledon on the opening day of the 1996–97 season and his profile on and off the pitch has made him one of the most recognised faces in world sport. An outstanding player, with a tremendous ability to take free kicks, and an inspirational captain.

## BEST, CLYDE

*Born: 24.02.51, Bermuda*

Clyde Best signed professional forms for West Ham United in 1969 and quickly became a favourite with the east-end fans. A big, bustling centre-forward in the old-fashioned mould, Best came to the fore at a time when foreign footballers were a rarity in the English game and the national side had yet to field a black player. After making his debut as an 18 year old in a 1–1 draw against Arsenal, Best appeared 187 times for the Hammers, scoring 47 goals.

## BOWYER, LEE

*Born: 3.1.77, Poplar*

Lee Bowyer's career has been dogged by controversy and he was involved in a high-profile court case in 2001 after an Asian student was beaten up in Leeds (Bowyer was aquitted). Even this could not prevent him from turning in a string of consistently good performances for Leeds that made Liverpool bid £9 million for him. After starting at Charlton he moved to Leeds for £2.6 million in 1996, becoming the most expensive teenager in the country. His off-the-field antics have captured more attention than his on-field exploits, but he is one of the best midfielders in the Premiership and a candidate for full England honours to add to a string of Under-21 caps. He can score vital goals and was a leading light in the Leeds side that reached the Champions League semi-final in 2001.

## BROWN, KEN

*Born: 16.2.1934, Dagenham*

Ken Brown joined West Ham as a professional at 17, making his debut in 1952. After National Service he went back to Upton Park and picked up a Second Division winner's medal in 1958. He won his sole England cap two years later in a 2–1 win over Northern Ireland. One of the less heralded members of Ron Greenwood's side which won the FA Cup and Cup-Winners' Cup in 1964 and 1965, Brown moved to Norwich in 1967 after 386 games for the Hammers. After ending his playing days at Hereford he became assistant manager to John Bond at Bournemouth in 1970 before the pair moved to Norwich in 1973. When Bond decamped to Manchester City, Brown took over in 1980. He won the Milk Cup in 1985 and a Second Division title. After a two-year spell managing Plymouth he left the game until Terry Venables made him an England scout in 1994.

## CAMPBELL, SOL

*Born: 18.9.1974, Newham*

Sol Campbell became one of the few players to cross the north London divide in 2001 when he moved from Tottenham to Arsenal on a Bosman free transfer. Campbell's availability on a free transfer sparked a European-wide chase for his signature but he chose to remain in London. The outcry sparked by the move was a testament to Campbell's talent as a centre-half and he helped his new side to the Premiership and FA Cup Double in his first season at Highbury. In nine years at Tottenham, Campbell won just one trophy, the Worthington Cup in 1999, when he captained the side. A regular for England since making his debut against Hungary in 1996, Campbell won his 50th cap in England's 3–0 win over Denmark at the 2002 World Cup. He scored his first goal for England in the tournament opener against Sweden.

## COLE, ASHLEY

*Born: 20.12.80, Stepney*

He has emerged as the best English left-back in the country, proving himself with Arsenal and then becoming an important part of the national team, a regular during the World Cup in Japan and South Korea. Cole had spent a loan spell at Crystal Palace before emerging into the full Arsenal side in 2000 with one appearance before making his mark the following year, and England recognition was not far away as he represented his country at youth level. His full debut came against Albania in 2001 and he has since become regarded as one of the best young players in the game. As a youngster he played for a club side called Puma, who regularly met Senrab, a team that included Ledley King of Spurs.

## CUNNINGHAM, LAURIE

*Born: 08.03.56, Archway*
*Died: 15.07.89*

Laurie Cunningham moved from Leyton Orient to West Bromwich Albion in 1977. Later that year he became the first black player to represent England at any level when he played for the Under-21s. He won six full caps.

His UEFA Cup quarter-final display against Valencia alerted Real Madrid, which, six months later, paid £950,000 to sign him. Despite scoring on his debut and contributing to Madrid's league and cup Double that year, he was sold in 1983. Cunningham then spent short spells at Marseilles, Manchester United, Sporting Gijon, Leicester City, Real Betis, Charleroi, Wimbledon and Rayo Vallecano. A second-half appearance in the 1988 FA Cup final earned Cunningham an FA Cup winner's medal but a year later he tragically died in a car crash just outside Madrid.

## GREAVES, JIMMY

*Born: 20.02.40, East Ham*

Jimmy Greaves made his Chelsea debut as a 17 year old against

Tottenham. It set the tone for his career – he scored. In his next four seasons Greaves scored 124 league goals before leaving for an ill-fated spell at AC Milan.

After scoring nine goals in 10 games for the Italians, he moved to Spurs for £99,999. Greaves finished top scorer three years running on his way to scoring 220 league goals in eight seasons at Spurs. He tasted success in the FA Cup (1962 and 1967) and the European Cup-Winners' Cup (1963) before moving to West Ham in 1969. He scored 13 goals there before retiring.

Despite a scoring record that would make him priceless in today's market, Greaves is still often remembered as the man who missed out when Sir Alf Ramsey's England lifted the World Cup in 1966.

## HURST, SIR GEOFF

*Born: 08.12.41, Ashton-under-Lyne*

Sir Geoff Hurst spent 13 seasons at West Ham, during which time the club won the FA Cup (1964) and the European Cup-Winners' Cup (1965). He scored 180 league goals in 411 games.

After an uncertain start Hurst began to find his feet in the top flight and became one of the most feared strikers in the league. In 1965–66 he finished the season as the league's top scorer with 40 goals.

Hurst is still the only man to score a hat-trick in a World Cup final but was actually a very late call-up to the squad. Ramsey ignored Hurst for England's group matches but an injury to Jimmy Greaves saw Hurst drafted in for the quarter-final against Argentina – which England won 1–0 courtesy of a trademark Hurst header. Despite widespread calls for Greaves's reinstatement, Hurst retained his place for the semi-final against Portugal – and the rest is history.

## INCE, PAUL

*Born: 21.10.67, Ilford*

Paul Ince made his name at West Ham as a tough, ball-playing midfielder but did not endear himself to the east-end fans when he chose to pose in a Manchester United shirt two weeks before his move to Old Trafford. The million-pound move in 1989 was the making of Ince and he won two Premierships, two FA Cups and a Cup-Winners' Cup before joining Inter Milan for £8 million in 1995. A key member of the England side that made the semi-finals of Euro '96, Ince returned to England in 1997 in a £4.2 million transfer to Liverpool. A big influence in England's progress to the 1998 World Cup, Ince fell out of favour with the England management, but a move to Middlesbrough in 1999 alerted Kevin Keegan's interest and he played in the Euro 2000 play-off win over Scotland and all three games in the subsequent championship. He has won 53 England caps, scoring twice.

## IZZETT, MUZZY

*Born: 31.10.74, Mile End*

Muzzy Izzett opted to play for Turkey in 2000 rather than England and was a member of the Turkish squad in the 2000 European Championships and 2002 World Cup. A right-footed midfielder, he started his career at Chelsea and graduated through the academy, cleaning Dennis Wise's boots on the way, but could not make a breakthrough. He joined Leicester on loan in April 1995 and quickly established himself in the side. He helped Leicester win the play-off final against Crystal Palace in 1995 and moved permanently to Filbert Street for £650,000. His goalscoring is a bonus; in the 2000–01 season he scored 11 times and although a year later he was again in double figures he could not help Leicester to avoid the drop.

## KING, LEDLEY

*Born: 12.10.80, Stepney*

Injuries have blighted a promising start to Ledley King's international career after he made a big impression in England's Under-21 European Championship in 2000 in Slovakia. King established himself at club level following the departure of Sol Campbell to Arsenal in 2001 and was rewarded with a place in the full England squad against Holland. He withdrew from the squad due to illness but made his full debut against Italy. Another injury ruled him out of 2002 World Cup contention. A fixture in the Spurs side, health permitting, he made his club debut in October 1999. Comfortable on the ball, he has many of the attributes of the man he replaced at White Hart Lane.

## LAMPARD, FRANK Snr
*Born: 20.9.1948, East Ham*

A solid defender who played for West Ham on 665 occasions, he was second behind Billy Bonds on the club's all-time list. He joined the club as a schoolboy apprentice when he was 15 and made the first team three years later. He won two FA Cup medals, in 1975 and 1980. Lampard was a reliable defender in his left-back role and one who could attack with effectiveness. When he left West Ham in 1985, he joined Bobby Moore at Southend as player-coach in the side managed by his former colleague. He returned to Upton Park in 1994 and enjoyed seven years at the club as No. 2 to Harry Redknapp. His son Frank Jnr, a midfielder, made his West Ham debut in 1996 and moved to Chelsea in July 2001.

## MOORE, BOBBY
*Born: 12.04.41, Barking*
*Died: 24.02.93*

Bobby Moore signed professional forms for West Ham in May 1958 and made his debut at the age of 17, against Manchester United, the following September. Widely regarded as the complete defender, Moore's name became a byword for skill, elegance and fair play. He made 642 appearances for West Ham, winning the FA Cup in 1964, when he was also named Footballer of the Year, and the European Cup-Winners' Cup in 1965. He led England to World Cup glory in 1966. The following year he was awarded the OBE. Moore won the first of his 108 England caps against Peru on 20 May 1962 and went on to captain his country on 90 occasions. His last England appearance came in a 1–0 defeat against Italy at Wembley in 1973. In 1974 Moore moved to Fulham, where he made 124 appearances and earned an FA Cup runners-up medal. On 24 February 1993 Bobby Moore died of cancer of the colon.

## PETERS, MARTIN
*Born: 8.11.43, Plaistow*

Despite enjoying a 20-year career as a professional, Peters is best known for his exploits as a youngster at West Ham. Snapped up after leaving school, the midfielder with an eye for the goal soon became a crowd favourite at Upton Park and forced his way into the England squad for the 1966 World Cup at the last minute. A goal in the final secured his place in history as England won the trophy, and also earned Peters the reputation of being a player ten years ahead of his time. Having won the European Cup-Winners' Cup with West Ham in 1965, Peters enjoyed more success at club level after moving to Tottenham in 1970. He helped Spurs to success in the League Cup in his first season, the UEFA Cup the following year and another victory in the League Cup in 1973. Peters moved on to Norwich in 1975 and enjoyed a short stay with Sheffield United before finally retiring in 1980 after winning 67 England caps and making 722 league appearances, scoring 174 goals.

## RAMSEY, ALF
*Born: 22.1.20, Dagenham*
*Died: 28.4.99*

While best remembered for his success in management, Ramsey was also a player of high pedigree. Nicknamed 'The General', he was a strong and quick right-back with a reputation for consistency. Ramsey won the first of 32 England caps with Southampton before a £21,000 fee took him to Tottenham in 1949. He missed just two matches over the next couple of seasons as Spurs won the Second and then the First Division titles. That successful touch was taken into management as Ramsey led Ipswich to three league championships – performances that earned him the England job. World Cup victory in 1966 ensured legendary status and a knighthood, though failure to qualify for the 1974 finals saw his career as national team manager end on a sour note.

## REDKNAPP, HARRY

Born: 2.3.47, Poplar

Harry played for West Ham 149 times during an 11-year career after joining the club in 1964. He went to Brentford and then Bournemouth, going back there in 1982 having caught the managerial bug. He then returned to West Ham in 1992. At first he was assistant to Billy Bonds and then a year later, he became manager with Frank Lampard Snr becoming his No 2. They had seven years at the club, Redknapp maintaining the theme of previous managers by making the place one of the most popular and welcoming clubs to go to in the country. In 1999, West Ham finished fifth in the Premiership, their best position in the top division for 13 years, but two seasons later, Redknapp left after the club just survived dropping into the first division. He then joined Portsmouth in June 2001 as director of football, before becoming manager of the south-coast club in March 2002.

## ROEDER, GLENN

*Born: 13.12.55, Woodford*

Glenn Roeder began his playing career at Leyton Orient before moving to QPR for £250,000. Under the guidance of Terry Venables, Roeder became a stylish centre-half and was part of the QPR team that reached the cup final in 1982. A year later Roeder moved to Newcastle, where he stayed for six years. He then had brief spells with Orient and Watford before taking over as player-manager at Gillingham. He left the Gills in 1993 to take over at Watford. In 1996 he left Vicarage Road and became part of Glenn Hoddle's England coaching team. He then worked as coach under Harry Redknapp at West Ham before taking over as manager in June 2001.

## SHERINGHAM, TEDDY

*Born: 2.4.66, Highams Park*

Teddy Sheringham was rated by the legendary Jurgen Klinsmann as the best footballing partner he ever had and the two had a profitable time at Tottenham during the German's time in London. Sheringham came to prominence as a striker with Millwall, scoring over 100 goals before a £2 million move to Nottingham Forest in 1991. He spent five years at Spurs after moving in 1992 but a desire to win trophies made him move to Manchester United in 1997. With Alan Shearer he had formed a potent strike-force for England and together they destroyed Holland in the 4–1 win in Euro '96. He won the Treble in 1999 scoring in both the FA Cup final and the Champions League final, and added a third Premiership title in 2000 before returning to Spurs. Another good season with Spurs saw him picked for the England World Cup squad at the age of 36.

## VENABLES, TERRY
*Born: 6.1.43, Dagenham*
Terry Venables played for England at every level from schoolboy upwards and made his name as a midfielder with Chelsea. A move to Tottenham saw him pick up an FA Cup-winners' medal in 1967 before he wound down his playing career at QPR and Crystal Palace. Coaching is his main strength and he won the Second Division with Crystal Palace and QPR before moving to Barcelona. He guided the Catalan club to the Spanish title in 1985 and to the European Cup final a year later. He returned to England with Tottenham in 1987 winning the FA Cup in 1991 before moving upstairs to become chief executive. After falling out with chairman Alan Sugar, he was sacked in 1993 but returned to coaching with England in 1994. England reached the semi-finals of Euro '96 under Venables, who took jobs with Portsmouth and Australia after the championships. Banned from being a director, he sold up his stake in Portsmouth and after a spell as coach back at Palace became a full-time TV pundit. He was tempted out of the studio by Leeds United in July 2002.

## ZAMORA, BOBBY
*Born: 16.1.81, Barking*
Bobby Zamora is one of the most sought-after strikers in the Football

League thanks to his goal-scoring exploits at Brighton, which have made him a cult hero on the South Coast. He started his career at Bristol Rovers in 1999 but was put on loan to Bath City in January 2000 and then to Brighton a month later. During his loan spell he scored six goals in six games, including a hat-trick against Chester, and the move was made permanent as Brighton forked out £100,000 for his services. The transfer fee looked a bargain in 2000–01 when Zamora scored 28 league goals as Brighton won the Third Division. A year later he repeated the trick as Brighton won the Second Division.

Biographical information supplied by and reproduced with kind permission of Hayters Sports Agency (0207 837 7171) or (0207 837 3400).